# In The Backwoods
# Of Nowhere

# Alma Cross Owen,
# her days recalled

*acknowledgements*

I would like to say a special thanks to my son-in-law, Don Wright, for his invaluable help with copyediting and for his kind encouragement.

*www.nancyblankenshipowen.com*

This is for my family, husband Glenn, who patiently waited over the years, hoping everyone who wanted to read this wouldn't die before I finished it—some did. And for my daughters Belinda Phillips, Jamie Chisholm, Laine Snyder and Glenna Wright who lovingly supported me in my efforts to put this book together.

Love, Hugs and Kisses,
Mom

# In The Backwoods Of Nowhere

## Alma Cross Owen,
### her days recalled

## Nancy Blankenship Owen

# an introduction

Alma's house was humming  with the usual horde of Sunday visitors. Many of her eleven children were there, some with spouses, some without. Scattered groups of grandchildren wondered about, and a few neighbors had come to sit and talk. I was there with my husband Glenn.

I found a seat in the living room. Not being an avid talker, I disappeared into the background; quietly watching the activity while I waited for the crowd to thin out. I had a request to ask of Alma, and I was nervous about approaching her with it. I didn't want to do it in front of people.

Alma has a way of making guests feel instantly at ease. When thinking of her home, I am reminded of a friends childhood experience that she reminisced to a group of us women at a church retreat some thirty years ago.

We were all sitting around on beds in pajamas, feet folded under us, giggling like a bunch of teenagers, listening as she told us that some of her fondest childhood memories were in Alma's home.

"When I was just a little girl, Mama took me visiting to Alma's house a lot. I liked going to Alma's. While Mama and Alma were busy talking together, I'd go off playing with the girls and I'd get to do things I didn't get to do at home because Mama was so strict.

On one visit, one of the girls took me into the kitchen to get a drink of water. When she opened the cabinet to get a glass I noticed the peanut butter jar setting inside on the shelf. It was open, with a knife sticking out of it—ready for anyone to just scoop out peanut butter and have it any time they wanted to. I thought that was heaven! Mama would never allow that at our house."

Alma's home is like that peanut butter jar—open and ready to enjoy anytime.


Alma is the perfect matriarch. A mere five foot three inches tall she displays a commanding presence. Through all the years I have known her, she has never ceased to amaze me.

A stout petite frame, crowned with soft white natural waves coifed about her face in a short neck length bob, grinning brown eyes beneath thick-lensed bifocal glasses, and a contagious soft chuckle sprinkled throughout her conversations, describe some of her amiable features. But her real charm lies not in her stature; it lies instead in her forever giving spirit and always optimistic persona.

Her incessant drive, even as she now moves toward her

nineties, and her never-ending fortitude in the face of any difficulty has been an inspiration to me over the years and causes me to question just what her secret is to surviving with such stamina.

As late afternoon arrived, I noticed that Glenn and I, along with a few straggling grandchildren, were the only ones left. So I pushed my apprehensions aside, got my courage up and said, "Mrs. Owen." I've always called her Mrs. Owen, have called her that for the forty-two years I've been her daughter-in-law. The other daughter-in-laws call her Alma or "maw maw," but the only words to address her that seem fitting to me are *Mrs. Owen.*

"Mrs. Owen, I've been thinking for some time now how little I know about your background—where you were born, how you grew up, how you met Odell."

She chuckled and nodded in agreement, knowing that she rarely talks about herself.

Then I said, "Would you be willing to tell me about your life experiences, with the intentions of me compiling them into a printed account of your life?"

I went on to explain to her how nice it would be for the family to have a written record for genealogy purposes.

She seemed pleased that I was interested and without hesitation, in her rural North Carolina accent, said, "Sure! Everybody's always been interested in hearing Odell. He's the one that did all the talking."

Odell, Alma's late husband, who died July 28, 1993 at age eighty-seven, was the family storyteller. He was a soft-spoken man of about five foot ten inches tall. He had dark blue-green eyes set back under thick brows and thinning salt and pepper hair that he combed back from the forehead. Farming was his life's work and his medium frame showed the wear of years of hard labor in the fields.

Odell had a passion for family history. His favorite pastime was reminiscing to family and friends about his days growing up on his daddy's farm, and about his ancestry. It was common on Sunday evenings to see groups of friends and relatives gathered around him in his living room bantering back and forth about *the good ole days* and comparing boyhood recollections.

I have a sense of acquaintance with Odell's ancestors because he not only told us about them, he made copies of old family photos and documents such as wills from past generations and passed them out to us so that we could enjoy a deeper knowledge of who they were and how they lived.

But I know very little to nothing about Alma's family history. I know that she has sisters and brothers, but have only met a few of them and barely know anything about them—just what I could find out from Glenn. I've heard her mention being raised in rural Davidson County, North Carolina, but don't know exactly where.

I want to know what her family life was like as a child, her experiences going to a country school, what it was like growing up as a young woman in the early 1900s in rural North Carolina. I want to know how she met Odell, their dating experiences and marriage and what it was like to birth and raise eleven children.

Alma's enthusiasm about the project was very encouraging. I

assured her of my interest and told her how sorry I was that I didn't think to do the same for Odell while he was living.

I told her I would like to start soon and suggested that for accuracy we tape record our conversations. She agreed.

A few days later, I phoned her to make plans for getting our project underway. She said the following morning around ten would be a good time for her.

Alma lives in a white brick house southwest of Lexington, North Carolina on the backside of what was originally hers and Odell's 275-acre farm. The country road that winds past her home serves as the western boundary for the farm and is dotted on both sides with houses, many belonging to her children and their families, mine included.

The next day, with heightened anticipation at the thought of having permission to delve into her past, I gathered up my notepad, tape recorder and a few other things I thought I might need, got in my car and made the short drive to Alma's house.

I turned into her graveled, tree-lined drive, and continued around to the back of the house coming to a stop beside the back porch. I grabbed my stuff and hurried to the door.

I was so excited, that without thinking I opened the door and went right on in—like I lived there. It shocked me that I did that. Alma's home *is* always open, and some *do* enter without knocking, but I was used to knocking first.

She evidently saw me coming, because she was standing just inside the door dressed in a blue pantsuit, her round softly lined face glowing with a big smile.

"Come on in," she said, as she motioned me inside.

"Well, I did," I said, and expressed my embarrassment at not knocking first.

She laughed her soft chuckle, pushed a stray piece of silver hair behind one ear and said, "You know you don't have to knock."

Her warm greeting eased my embarrassment and made me feel right at home.

After wiping my feet on a rug just inside the door, I followed her through a short utility entrance hall into the kitchen, a far cry, I imagined, from the one she started out in when she and Odell were first married.

Alma's kitchen, roomy and equipped with all the modern conveniences, was filled with the aroma of fresh baked chicken pies cooling on the counter. She pointed to them and said for me to take one home for supper when I leave. I quickly thanked her, mouth watering in anticipation of cutting into it at suppertime.

Cooking is one of Alma's favorite pastimes, which is fortunate for us—her family and friends—because she is constantly sharing her goodies with us. But her sharing doesn't stop with us. It extends to all the critters in her yard through her numerous animal and bird feeders. She likes to watch the birds feed on her treats through the window over her sink as she cooks.

Opposite the kitchen sink and next to a large refrigerator freezer, a desktop area displays a massive photo collage of faces—children, grandchildren and great grandchildren—that Alma proudly adds to as new faces are born into the family.

She never forgets a birthday. She sends everyone's birthday to the local radio station to be announced on the air in a birthday contest drawing for a free cake and other gifts from local merchants. We all look forward to it. There are so many of us, someone is always winning.

From the kitchen, she led me through her elegantly furnished dining room into her spacious living room—the two rooms being one large open area painted a soft ivory.

On the far end of the living room, in front of a large picture window, sat a pair of burgundy upholstered chairs separated by a table displaying some of her meticulously groomed flowers and plants. The window gave view of the front porch and wooded front yard, and ushered in soft morning sunlight that illuminated the room. A gas heater setting on the raised hearth of her fireplace provided warmth from the chill of the late October day.

I sat down in front of the fireplace on her beige and brown tweed sofa and placed my notepad beside me. Alma sat to my right in her black leather recliner, her usual resting place.

While I positioned the tape recorder on a small table between us, we conversed about the family, the beautiful fall day and her gorgeous potted plants—me saying how I wish I could grow them as easily as she seemed to be able to.

Then, I asked her if she was ready for our journey back in time. She chuckled softly, pushed back in her recliner to lift her feet a little and said, "yes!"

Anxious not to miss a single word, I reached over, pushed the record button and our journey began.

This was the first of many visits sitting at Alma's side immersed in stories of days gone by. A way of life that I envied at certain times and at other times glad I was born in a more modern age.

I will now share with you, in her own rural North Carolina voice, this rare and beautiful woman's life account; with hopes of providing a deeper insight into her person and the times in which she lived.

# In The Backwoods Of Nowhere

## Alma Cross Owen,

### her days recalled

# 1

Odell and me were married sixty-four years when he died. We had seven boys and four girls; all living now except one, Macks. He died after Odell did at age sixty-two.

On our fiftieth wedding anniversary the children gave us a party here at the house. Odell called a photographer. They made pictures of Odell and all the boys, but they didn't make pictures of the girls or any of Odell and me together.

I said, "It's my anniversary!"

But he didn't have my picture made. So my brother Fred called a photographer back out here a few days later and had some made. They made pictures of Odell and me together and some of the girls, what we could get together. On our sixtieth anniversary we went up to Foy and Shirley's house, our oldest son and his wife, that live about ten miles north of us in Midway. All the children were there. They gave us a big vase of roses.

Front row from left to right: Foster, Linda, Doug, Fay and Kay
Back row from left to right: Glenn, Hazel, Odell, Tommy, Alma, Kenneth, Macks, Foy

Odell and me were both born and raised right here in Davidson County, North Carolina. It's a pretty place to live. It's made up mostly of beautiful rolling wooded hills with plenty of rich farmland. We're situated in the piedmont triad or central part of North Carolina, along with Winston-Salem to the north of us in Forsyth County, and Greensboro and High Point to the northeast in Guilford County.

Davidson County is shaped kind of like a triangle—wide at the top where the northern portion joins Davie and Forsyth Counties, then going down to a point at the bottom where we meet Montgomery County. We're one of the largest counties in the state acreage wise. We have two main cities, Lexington, the county seat, with a population of a little over thirty thousand, and

Thomasville, about the same size, located ten miles to the northeast. Denton, a smaller town, about ten percent of the population of Lexington, is sixteen miles or so south on Highway 109. The rest of the county is made up of numerous small rural communities, with names such as Reeds, Tyro, Churchland, Linwood, Cotton Grove, Healing Springs, Southmont, Lick Creek, High Rock, Newsom, Jackson Hill and many, many more.

In the 1800s and early 1900s when travel was slow, mainly by horse, or horse and wagon, a trip to town came only a few times a year. That made these small communities necessary to the survival of the nearby farmers and their families. Each community had its own general store, school and church. The general store supplied needed goods to the farmers that they couldn't grow or make themselves.

Then cotton mills and factories, such as furniture making, started cropping up in nearby towns. Travel became much easier and faster with the coming on of the passenger train and automobile. So men started leaving these outlying communities and the farming way of life to work in the factories, hoping for a better and easier living. Lexington and Thomasville are now known all over the world for their furniture making.

Odell was born September 28, 1905 to John David, (JD) and Martha Eliza Snider Owen. He grew up five to six miles south of Lexington in the Linwood community on his daddy's farm.

Linwood didn't have a school at the time, so he was educated to the eighth grade in a one-room school in the near-by Center Hill community. They went by the books at Center Hill and the eighth grade was as much as you could get in that school.

They closed the Center Hill School and built a new school in Linwood that went to higher grades, but Odell didn't want to go back to school. So he wouldn't go.

At the old Center Hill School, when school was out in the spring they would have a celebration. They would give a little play or something and they called it *The Exhibition*. I went there one time to *The Exhibition*. I went with my sister Julie and one of her boyfriends. I don't remember how old I was at the time, but we had already moved to Lexington.


I was born in lower Davidson County June 28, 1910 to Nancy Caroline Taylor Cross and Stephen Harris Cross. We lived fifteen miles or so south of Lexington off number 8 Highway, down between Newsom and High Rock, near Jackson Hill and Bald Mountain—in the backwoods of nowhere.

Now-a-day Newsom, High Rock and Jackson Hill are almost unheard of. Old abandoned general stores and a few stately houses are all that's left to mark their existence and tell of the way we lived.

We were, for the most part, cut off from neighboring towns. A trip to Lexington by horse-drawn wagon, which was all Daddy had at the time, took from sun up 'til sun down. Us kids walked to wherever we went, to school or to nearby settlements or to

4

wherever else. These days, people stick up their noses at such, but they'll go way up to the Amish country in Pennsylvania to view the Amish people ride in their wagons and buggies and doing their work the old way.

Occasionally, when somebody would happen to go to Lexington for somethin' nother they would come back telling stories. Stories about seeing a car, and I would wonder, what is a car? I never saw a car. We didn't know what cars was.

The first airplane I ever saw looked just about like a bird in the sky. I can remember during the time of the First World War, we would hear a little roar and they would say, "It's an airplane!" and everybody would get out and look to see if they could see an airplane. Sometimes you could see a little speck and sometimes you couldn't. But that was entertainment for us.

The Southbound and the Southern Railroads were the two main railroads that ran through the county. A smaller railroad called the HPT&D, or High Point, Thomasville and Denton, ran from High Point to High Rock. I think it mostly carried supplies and freight. The Southern and the Southbound carried passengers.

The Southern railroad ran east from Salisbury to Linwood, then to Lexington, and on through Thomasville. The Southbound ran south from Winston-Salem to Lexington, then down through the county to High Rock and on by Bald Mountain—between the mountain and the Yadkin River—then it went through Newsom and continued fifteen miles south to Albemarle in Stanly County.

The Southbound was completed in 1910. Mama said they

5

were building on the railroad when I was a baby, but I was too little to remember that.

Newsom, at the foothills of Bald Mountain, was our gathering place. It had a Southbound Railroad depot where trains came and went on a regular schedule. They picked up passengers, picked up freight and all that. There was a general store, a sawmill up on the side of the mountain, a broom factory and a rock quarry. We could hear the blasting at the quarry from where we lived, a way up between Newsom and High Rock. They used the rock to put on the roads and things. It used to be a big business.

There was a number of houses around the settlement, some large some small and the old Fredonia School was up the road a good ways.

One year when the typhoid fever was so bad they started giving shots, so families would meet at Newsom and get their shots. Mama said my brother Irvin had it when he was small, but he survived it.

People would come to Newsom to go by train to Lexington and Albemarle to get jobs in the cotton mills, hosiery mills and furniture factories, especially young people. The young people would board in town during the week and come home by train on the weekend.

High Rock was smaller than Newsom. It was maybe three or more miles north of Bald Mountain, but not far to walk when you go down the railroad. High Rock was just a small community of houses and a general store.

Jackson Hill was about five miles east of Newsom on the

other side of Highway 8. They had a church with a graveyard—most all the churches had graveyards—a general store, a post office, and a doctor's office. Just a little country village.

Before the Southbound Railroad was built, Jackson Hill had been a big settlement with hopes of getting bigger. When plans for the railroad were being made, they thought that it was coming through their village. They looked forward to the railroad bringing jobs and more people to Jackson Hill and it growing like Lexington, but when they built the railroad, they decided to run it along the Yadkin River through Newsom instead. The railroad attracted people to Newsom, so Newsom became the head-quarters.

$$\mathscr{P}$$

I was the fifth of nine children, two boys and seven girls. Irvin was the oldest; he's eleven years older than me. After Irvin comes Julie, she's nine years older than me, then Lela, five years older, then Virgie, three years older. I come after Virgie, then Frances, I'm two years older than Frances and four years older than Fred. Fred is four years older than the twins Cora and Flora. They were the babies. Mama had one baby boy, that came somewhere between us, that died at birth.

Flora, Virgie and me are the only ones still living out of the nine.

Mama named me Alma Lee. I have no idea who I was named after. I think *Alma* was someone Mama knew when she was young or something. The Lee was just added on. I don't know what or who in particular; I don't know of anybody named that. It's just the L double E.

When I was small I was short and kind of chubby with a round face. Mama called me "Duck." She said I kind of waddled when I walked. Nobody called me by that but Mama. I had dark, almost black, naturally wavy hair like Daddy's that Mama kept cut in a bob just below my ears. Mama didn't have time to take care of long hair. Irvin had dark hair too. The other girls and Fred took after Mama with fair skin and lightish brown hair. Cora and Flora's hair was white when they were small.

From left to right: Lela, Alma, Daddy, Irvin, Virgie, Mama, Julie

I remember the house they said I was born in. It was an old timey house. The living room was Mama and Daddy's bedroom, and then some little bedrooms to the side. It had a breezeway, a kitchen and a dining room. There was a grape arbor in the back yard. I vaguely remember seeing the arbor. They said I had the whooping cough while I lived there. They said that when I'd get started coughing I would run out and grab the grapevine. I don't know what I thought that would do, but that's what they used to laugh and tell me.

I've often wondered what it looks like down there now, and if I'd go to those places if I could find anything or not.

In the 1950s the Aluminum Company of America bought land to build Tucker Town reservoir and dam in the southern tip of Davidson County. The dam was finished in the 60s and backed up water over most of Newsom. The place I was born is not under water now, but the way to get to it is. The water came up and closed off the road.

# 2

I must have been about four years old when Mama sent me to stay with Daddy's Uncle Burl and Aunt Ellen Skeen that lived between Newsom and Jackson Hill. They had four grown children, two girls, Ruth and Carrie, and two boys, Forest and John.

The two boys were off fighting in the First World War, the two girls lived at home. Ruth and Carrie both worked in Albemarle in the hosiery mill. They rode the Southbound train and boarded down there during the week.

Ruth and Carrie loved children so they would borrow one of Mama's children to look after. My older sister, Virgie, said she stayed one time, but I was too little to remember that.

Ruth and Carrie wore their dresses down to their ankles—that was the style—and had long brown hair that they combed up into a ball on the back of their head. I don't know how old they were,

10

but they called them old maids. Later on, Ruth got married, but Carrie never did. I thought they were pretty girls, but I was real small at the time.

Aunt Ellen, she had long dark hair too that she wore up in a ball on the back of her head. Most women wore their hair like that—a ball on the back of their head or a ball on top of their head. Aunt Ellen wasn't a heavy woman, just an ordinary size.

Uncle Burl was a medium sized man with a potbelly. I remember him having dark hair and a chin beard. I guess I was too little to remember much else about him.

Aunt Ellen and Uncle Burl lived in a plain unpainted two-story frame house with weatherboarding on it. The kitchen, living room and a bedroom were on the lower floor. The top floor had two more bedrooms. That's where I slept.

Next to the kitchen was a partition with a little breezeway and we would sit out there in the summer time to get the breezes. I don't know whether he rented the house or owned it. I always thought he owned it, but I don't know for sure.

Ruth and Carrie were so good to me. While I was there, they were the ones that really took care of me. They treated me just like a queen. Those girls bought me the prettiest clothes. They would buy the clothes in Albemarle where they worked and bring them to me.

Once, Ruth and Carrie bought me a dress that had little white bands on the sleeves and a white collar. It buttoned up the front and gathered at the waist. Boy, I thought I was a queen. I was a doll I reckon to Ruth and Carrie.

Most of the time Ruth and Carrie would both be off working in Albemarle together, but sometimes one would be home, while the other was off working, but most of the time, they were off working together. When they were in for the weekend, they would sleep upstairs with me, but when they were both in Albemarle working, I slept up there by myself. A lot of children would have been scared, but I wasn't.

Ruth took me with her on the train to Albemarle—I think I went twice down there—and we stayed overnight in the house where she boarded. A little girl in the house—she had tuberculosis. They didn't say anything about it being catching. Later on, the little girl sent me a picture about four inches tall of a cupid. I still got it hanging in my bedroom. I don't know how I kept it all them years or where I kept it or where Mama kept it for me, but I've still got it. It's at least 86 or 87 years old now. Years later I started keeping things in something I called my treasure box. I wouldn't take anything for that picture.

One weekend Ruth and Carrie took me on the train to Lexington to stay with Daddy's brother, Tom. Sunday morning, they took me to town to the First Baptist Church. At that time First Baptist was on South Main Street where the gas company is now. Some years later they built a big new church on West Third Avenue.

I had probably been to the country churches with Mama and Daddy, but I had never been to a large church like First Baptist.

There in the church I noticed a woman a-breast-feeding her child. Her child was about as old as I was, and she was still a-nursing her mama. I thought that was something awful.

Ruth and Carrie took me on to my Sunday school class and gave me some money to put in the collection plate, but I didn't know to put it in. I took it home with me. I never had any money before. They didn't scold me or nothing. They just said I should have put it in; they knew I didn't know to. Ruth and Carrie were just country girls, but they had gone back and forth to Albemarle and had attended a big church down there. I didn't know nothing about that.

Aunt Ellen was good to me, but being a child I could be playful at times. Like, one day when Daddy's nephew Lee and his wife Nannie that lived in Lexington came down with their children to visit. Their oldest girl was close to my age so we went out in the yard under a tree to play. Aunt Ellen had a little flower garden out there and the Sweet Williams was a-bloomin. That's the flower that looks like a little carnation bloom. So I went and picked them and gave them to that little girl. I know Aunt Ellen didn't like it, but I didn't know not to pick them.

Uncle Burl had a gray cat. He said it was to catch the rats. Well, one evening Aunt Ellen sent me upstairs to take a nap and the cat went with me.

One thing people always said was, if you throwed a cat down it will always land on its feet. So, I wasn't sleepy, and I got

13

irritated about somethin' nother and I thought about that saying.

"So well," I said to myself, "I'm going to see whether it does or not."

So I took the cat and I throwed it down. It landed on its feet that time. I throwed it down another time, and it landed on its back. It knocked it out for a little while. So, they don't always land on their feet. I was experimenting.

Uncle Burl had apple trees and made apple cider. He took a little keg with a spigot on it and filled it up with cider just for me. Aunt Ellen let me make a playhouse out under a tree in the yard and Uncle Burl set my keg out there under the tree on a couple of rocks or somethin' nother. I'd sit out there in my playhouse and drink my cider. It was fun. I felt real special. I thought that was real cute after I got old enough to remember it.

On my sixth birthday, Uncle Burl went plowing in the field with his mule. I don't know what he was planting, corn or something. He wasn't in good health at the time. He had a cancer on his face and he wasn't feeling good at all. Aunt Ellen told me to go along with him; I guess it was to get me out of the way, and maybe in case anything happened to him, I could come back and tell them. So, I went along. I took a little bucket and while he was working I picked blackberries. I picked the little bucket full and ate some too. Aunt Ellen made pies out of them.

That was my sixth birthday.

Aunt Ellen's house was a couple miles or so from the old Fredonia School house. So, that fall I went to school my first half-year at Fredonia from Aunt Ellen's.

I walked. Everybody walked. Everybody I went to school with lived a couple miles or so from the school.

I remember a little girl named Katherine Stokes. Katherine was my first friend. We didn't go from one house to another to play like children do now because all the houses were too far apart, but I walked to Katherine's house some to play. Her house was on the way to school and I'd walk over to her house and walk to school with her and her brother.

Later on, Katherine's family moved to Linwood. After she moved I don't remember talking to her anymore. Years later I learned that after she grew up she married a man from Midway, a small community up near Winston-Salem, and lived up there until she died.

Fredonia was a two-room school. The younger ones had classes in one room, and then after they got up to the fourth or fifth grade, they went over to the other room. That way it kept the larger ones separated from the little. They couldn't aggravate the little ones and the little ones couldn't aggravate them.

Every morning Aunt Ellen would fix my lunch to carry to school. My favorite was fried bread. She would make the dough, and I'd help roll it out, then she'd cut it and fry it in the pan and make little sticks of fried bread. I loved that.

Every morning Aunt Ellen would say, "Alma, what do you

want to take to school for lunch today?"

"Fried bread." I'd say.

"You got to eat something else," she'd say, "They going to think all we got is fried bread for you."

She would fix me ham or sausage, but I would rather have fried bread. I don't remember just how I carried it; we didn't have paper bags. I guess she just wrapped it up in somethin' nother.

That Christmas, I remember them having a little Christmas program. They put all us beginners together. All the little girls had dolls; I don't remember what the boys had. We had a song to sing to our dolls. We'd hold our dolls and sing to them, then we'd lay them down, then we'd go back, pick our dolls up, hold them and sing to them. I have no idea what the song was. I can remember that we sung to them, but can't remember what we said or anything. I'd like to remember that song, something about putting my doll to bed.

After Christmas Mama came and took me home.

The time I spent with Aunt Ellen and Uncle Burl and Ruth and Carrie was one of the happiest times of my life. I can still remember things they did and so on.

That fall Mama and me went and pulled corn for a man. He had a big field just past where Daddy was farming. We pulled corn all day long for them to get ready for the corn shucking.

At the end of the day, they paid Mama and she gave me a dollar, said, "That's what you made a-pulling corn."

That's the first money I remember earning. That was a lot of money then. I guess I pulled pretty good. I always liked doing things like that; so I earned my dollar.

Mama took the dollar and bought material and made me a pretty dress. It was a plaid with lots of blue and some red. It wasn't a dressy dress like Ruth and Carrie bought me; it was a school dress.

I thought that was something. I'd worked and bought my dress.

# 3

The first house I remember much about was when we moved from the house I was born in, across Cabin Creek to a little shack on the Reid farm. The Reid farm laid between where Cabin Creek and Lick Creek flowed into the Yadkin River and was built up by Raymond Reid back in the 1800s.

The Reid farmhouse was a large two-story white clapboard. They said it was partly built by slave labor. I went to the Reid house visiting one time. I don't remember who was with me, maybe Mama or her younger sister, Aunt Bessie; I was real small.

One of Reid's married girls was there—took us around, and showed us through the house. I remember it being just a typical old colonial house. I was too little to notice much about the furnishings, but I would think it had fine furniture for that time.

They had their own blacksmith shop, sawmill, and smoke-houses. They say at one time it even had a gristmill. They had what they called a tramping barn, used as a threshing room to thresh grain; the only one like it in the southeast.

I remember the tramping barn. It was built up two stories high. Horses were led up a ramp to the upper room where they were led around over opened shocks of grain that were scattered over the floor. The walking loosened the grain from the chaff. The floorboards were separated some so the loosened grain could fall between the cracks to the grain room below.

The grain room had something like bins pulled up on the sides so the grain couldn't get away after it fell down there. Men would scoop the grain up and toss it in the air to wind it out— remove any left over chaff—or do what ever else was needed.

They used the tramping barn to thresh the wheat when we first moved there. Threshing machines came along later—at first they used the tramping barn.

Daddy sharecropped for the Reid's. Sharecropping is where you work another man's land for a share. After the Civil War, sharecropping became a way of life in the Southeast for farmers who didn't own land. If a farmer had his own farming equipment and horses, he got two thirds of the crop and the landowner got a third. If the landowner furnished the equipment then it's turned around; the farmer got a third and the landowner got two thirds for owning the land and the livestock. Daddy owned his own equipment and livestock.

Daddy grew wheat and corn for shares. Besides that, he grew all our vegetables, some peanuts, cotton and a little tobacco.

19

He wasn't the only sharecropper on the Reid farm. We farmed on one side of a creek and another family farmed the other side.

Daddy went out early in the morning to work the fields. He plowed with a horse-drawn plow one furrow at a time. At that time everybody worked the fields with horses or mules; nobody had a tractor. That was unheard of then.

Besides working the fields, he had to gather hay to feed the animals. He'd gather enough hay during the spring and summer months to feed them through the winter.

A big field near our house had clover sowed in it and it would get up high. We loved to get out there and play and hide in it; we had lots of fun playing in it. When Daddy got ready to mow the clover, he'd have to run us out.

He'd holler, "You kids get out of there!"

And we'd have to quit playing so he could mow.

Daddy mowed it with his horse-drawn mower. Then he stored the hay in haystacks so it would save.

To make the haystacks, he'd take a pole and set it in the ground. Then he packed the loose hay around the pole 'til it got up as high as he wanted it. He'd let some of them get real high. He rounded the top so the rain would run off. That way the hay underneath would keep from spoiling.

The cows ate from the haystacks by just going around the stack a-eating on it. They'd eat it from the bottom, and as they'd eat, the hay would slide down the pole from the top so they'd get the top last.

Daddy was lucky if he found enough good hay to last through

the winter. Sometime he'd run out of the good hay and have to feed off the sagebrush. Sagebrush was all right for a little while, but it didn't have the strength in it that the good hay did.

It was a hard life. Daddy didn't have nobody to help him. When Irvin got big enough to do anything, he left home and went off to do public work. He was no more than fourteen or fifteen when he left.

He got a job in Knoxville, Tennessee laying pipe—doing aluminum pipefitting; he made good money. He helped out at home with part of his income. Back then you were expected to help.

Our house was on the side of a hill, with the kitchen part built directly against the ground—in fact, in the ground. The land was fixed so the water wouldn't run into the house when it came down the hill during a rain.

The kitchen and dining room were together, then three bedrooms were built to the side of the hill going up the mountain. One bedroom was used as a sitting room too. We were piled up. It was just a small house.

On the side next to the valley, we had a porch that we had no way of getting to from the outside, no steps built up to it. It was about seven foot up off the ground with a banister around it. We went in and out of the house from the backside at the kitchen.

We used to sit on the porch to string beans, talk and relax in the summer time—when we had time. I can remember playing on the porch and climbing out the banisters. It's a wonder we hadn't a-fell off and broke our neck. People fuss about children doing dangerous things now, and I think about the things that I did.

We got our water for cooking and bathing from a spring, a place where water flows up naturally from the ground. At that time most everybody got their water from springs or wells. Our spring was up the hill above our house. To take baths we'd carry water from the spring and heat it on the woodstove in the kitchen. We'd bathe one at a time in a washtub—in the same bath water. It was too hard to tote the water for all of us to have private baths. 'Course we didn't take baths every day.

Mama would go up to the spring to do her washing. She had the wash pot and tubs up there. She had to carry the clothes up there, scrub them by hand, then carry them back down to the house to put them on the line to dry. Nobody knows how lucky they are now. Mama lived hard.

From that house, Daddy moved us into one of Reid's houses over on the other side of the mountain. It had a pretty good-sized barn.

It was just an ordinary unpainted two-story farmhouse. None of the houses we lived in were painted inside or out. We didn't know what paint was. They were just plain board houses.

The house was built on the side of a hill in kind of an open area, and of course the mountain went on up. A winding road came past the barn, then went by the house and on down the valley. It was more like a path than a road, a one-lane thing, just a wagon road, just nothing but wagons and buggies then no how.

There were two small bedrooms upstairs, kind of like attic rooms, and two bedrooms downstairs, then the dining room and kitchen all together. We had an L shaped porch that came around from the kitchen, turned and went across the front. There were two little rooms built off the porch with doors to go in them from the porch.

We had a fireplace in the kitchen where we did some of the cooking. The kitchen didn't have cabinets like they do now, just a couple of small tables and maybe some shelves for dishes and things.

We never had a toilet. Mama had Daddy to fix her a seat out in the woods between two small trees; 'course it was growed up around it so you couldn't see. So that's where she would go and we'd just go where ever we could out in the bushes. It was quite different—more healthy. But it's no wonder everybody had typhoid fever and all.

We used leaves for toilet paper. We had to be careful we didn't get a hold of one with a worm on it. Some of the bushes had stinging worms that would go on them. You had to look at them before you used them.

At night, we used a pot and the next day we emptied it in the woods. We were in the wilderness. That's why I said, *in the backwoods of nowhere.* But we had fun. We didn't know the danger.

# 4

Daddy called mama Nannie; everybody called her that. She called him Harris.

Daddy was born September 12, 1877 in High Rock, to Mary and Peter Cross. Mama was born July 29, 1879 to Frances and Alexander Taylor on their farm near Cabin Creek.

I have no idea how Mama and Daddy met. I never heard nobody say. My older sisters never talked about that. They were probably married by the Justice of the Peace. That's the way everybody got married back then, unless they were what we called, *rich people.* They'd have a big wedding.

Mama was short, about five feet three inches and a little on the heavy side. Daddy was slim, average height—slightly taller than Mama—just ordinary. Mama's hair was long and curly-like. She wore it up in a ball on the back of her head and would put combs and hairpins around in it for decoration. Daddy wore his hair parted and combed to the side.

None of the women cut their hair. That was just a tradition among all the women. They believed a woman wasn't supposed to cut her hair because the Bible says not to. They thought you was a whore if you cut your hair.

There was a family that lived down toward Healing Springs, a community a little north of us, and the woman was a redhead. She had her hair cut off real short and everybody said she was just a whore. Everybody made fun of her. It was long hair, long dresses and high top shoes or you was talked about. So everybody had long hair, except the men of course. Somebody in the family or somebody in the neighborhood usually cut the men's hair.

Daddy was clean-shaven; I don't remember Daddy ever having a chin beard or mustache, but a lot of men did. It was the style. Daddy shaved with a straight razor that he kept sharp with a leather strap he had hanging on the wall. He used the strap to sharpen all the knives and anything that needed sharpening.

Daddy wore overalls for his everyday work clothes and he most always wore some kind of hat. But when he wasn't working, he'd have on his suit and dress hat. All the men dressed like that. When they weren't working, they were dressed up, that was the way. Daddy bought his suits and his work clothes in Newsom at the general store. They weren't expensive. The High Rock general store sold them too, but Daddy bought his in Newsom.

Mama made all her clothes—high neck dresses down to her ankles. Women never wore pants. That was another no no. She didn't have any jewelry, except maybe a dress pin. I don't remember her having a wedding ring.

Women wore aprons over their dresses most of the time, so if something got dirty, it was the apron. Mama wore the band apron around the waist—from the waist down. Some women wore the bib kind that covered the chest. If somebody came visiting, Mama would take her apron off and put it aside.

Mama didn't wear lipstick or anything like that. Using make-up was another bad thing, but some girls would take that red crepe decorating paper and rub it on their lips to make them red. They'd get a hold of a piece, rub it on their lips, and some of them got sores from that. It wasn't pure. Some of them would have their cheeks all red too. I don't know what they used for rouge, probably that red paper. Some of them put flour on their face for powder. It would make them look awful white. People used just what they could get a hold of. We didn't have make-up like they do now.

Mama made all our clothes too, even our underwear. She bought cotton cloth and made panties that were down to our knees, sort of like the shorts that the girls wear now. She didn't have elastic, so she'd put a little button at the waistline, or we'd pin them to keep them up. She made them near to fit, but not too tight.

She made the boys underwear too. She couldn't buy the boys long underwear as cheap as she could get the cloth and make them. Theirs went on down their leg further than ours.

She'd make our slips, and of course our dresses. If I ever had a bought dress I don't remember—except for the ones Ruth and Carrie bought me. Our stockings?—we bought them at the general store.

When us girls got big enough that our breast started growing, we'd just take a piece of cloth, just a straight piece of cloth and tie it around us and pin it. It would be pinned so it would be fitted at the top and the bottom like a bra, but it didn't hold up like a bra.

I was living in town when I started growing and you could buy bras then, but I didn't buy them. The cloth worked just as well.

Mama made our dresses to come down to just around our ankles. We did all our playing in our dresses. We weren't allowed to wear pants like the boys, it made it hard playing. Of course our dresses were flared out, but it didn't make it any easier running or playing baseball or climbing a tree.

We wore the same clothes in the summertime that we wore in the wintertime. Except in the summertime we didn't wear the real thick ones and we didn't wear stockings; we went barefooted.

We'd get a new pair of shoes in the fall for school. As they wore out Daddy would repair them. He had a shoe last and he'd buy the leather and tacks and in his spare time or at night he'd put new soles on them if they wore out during the winter.

My shoes were usually black or brown. They came up to the ankle like the boys'. One pair I had, had a metal cap on the toe like the boys. They didn't wear out so easy that way. They usually lasted all winter.

My older sisters, Julie and Lela, wore high top shoes. They buttoned way up the leg. They came with a little hook to pull the buttons through. I thought they were something. They went out of style before I got old enough to wear them.

One time somebody gave us a bunch of used shoes. I got a pair with a heel about an inch and a half high. They were nice looking, but they didn't fit me right. I wore them anyway because I thought they were so pretty. One day a bunch of us went walking up to High Rock Mountain for somethin' nother and so I wore those shoes. They made blisters and about ruined my feet.

# 5

Daddy was a hard worker and was always good to us kids. Mama was too. As far as I know they never fussed or anything—just easy going. Mama liked to be the leader, so she kind of took the lead in everything. Mama made the decisions in what was what and what we bought. Growing up, Daddy was the baby of his family; his brothers and sisters were all grown when he was born. They told stories about how as a boy Daddy was always petted and didn't have any management.

Mama wasn't a good manager of money either. If she got any money, there was always a hole to put it in. She wanted things she didn't have and would buy things when she didn't need it. Sometimes that made it hard, but Daddy just took it and went on. He never tried to force his will on her—or anybody.

One time, a man come around selling phonographs—talking machines. Mama got one and kept it there a little while. People would come in to hear our talking machine. It was one of those little Victrolas that had the horn on top. It was interesting. I think sometimes now about how it sounded—a lot different than they do now.

We didn't have it long before he came back and took it because she couldn't pay for it. I don't know why the man let her keep it. She wanted it a whole lot. While it was there we didn't dare touch it. If we'd a-damaged it somebody would have had to pay for it.

Mama buying things she didn't need and couldn't pay for—some children would take a big notice of that, but I never did. I just took everything for granted.

She bought a pump organ one time. Most everybody that could afford one had one. Mama got hers secondhand from somebody that was getting rid of it. She liked music. She practiced on it, but she never learned to play. I guess she never had time to really get down to business. We'd play on it, but we didn't learn how to make a tune or anything.

Daddy didn't have any interest in the organ; he played the harmonica some. He would sit around at night and play the ole timey songs, a hoedown, or something like that and Mama and Daddy would sing.

Sometimes Daddy sang when he'd be in the fields a-working. He'd sing songs like "Old Dan Tucker," and "Old Black Joe" and things like that.

Daddy was a good man and wouldn't bother nobody, but he'd

take up for something he believed in. He was very strong in his ideas and all. One time somebody was arguing politics with him and it made him mad. They were throwing off on the Republican politics, and he didn't like that one bit. I don't like them throwing off on one another either. So maybe I took that from him.

Daddy went to Jackson Hill and voted every time it came time to. Mama couldn't vote. Women didn't vote then. They didn't get to vote 'til along about the 1920s—about the time we moved to Lexington. Mama wasn't a political person; didn't care to vote. But when the vote came in for women, she'd go along with Daddy and vote. Most of the men didn't take their wives to vote, but Daddy took Mama every time.

Daddy's parents, Mary and Peter Cross, lived right at the foot of High Rock Mountain—right under the big rock. High Rock was just a great big rock hanging up on the side of the mountain. It was big as some of the houses. It reaches up, I don't know how far—great long. When they cut the timber off the mountain you could see it better. Now the leaves cut the view of it.

As a young girl, I used to play on High Rock Mountain. Us kids had a path that went up to the rock. We used to catch on to bushes or anything we could use to pull ourselves up. When we got up to the rock we could see all over the countryside. It was pretty.

Going down was harder than going up. Going down, we'd

hold on to small sapling growing along the path to keep from sliding.

Daddy didn't come from a large family, but I guess it may be considered large by today's standards. He had three brothers, Jim, Tom and Eli and three sisters, Ruth, Clarinda and Charity. I never knew Daddy's sisters. They were all a lot older than Daddy, and lived fourteen miles or so west of us in Salisbury. Eli lived over there too. Jim and Tom lived in Lexington.

None of them farmed. They all went to town to work. That's another reason I never knew them much.

Uncle Tom was an overseer in a furniture factory. We came up on the train and visited him once or twice. His girls thought we weren't good enough for them.


Daddy had an average education. He must have gone to school somewhere around High Rock—what school he went. He could write and read well and he could figure too. He was good at that. Mama could read and write, but Daddy was better with his than she was. Back then they didn't send the girls to school as much as they did the boys. They didn't care too much about sending the boys either, they only went to school four or five months a year. They had to mind the farm. Work was more important—that was their motto.

Daddy used to read to us some, but we didn't have much to read from. Sometimes we would have a magazine that somebody gave us, but mostly all we had to read was our schoolbooks, the Bible and the almanac.

The almanac was a necessity. The almanac and the Bible were the two main books people had. They went by the signs in the almanac for everything. They planted their fields raised their chickens and bred their animals all by the almanac. They even had their teeth pulled by it. It tells in the almanac a good time to have teeth pulled and all.

I still buy the almanac, 'cause I like to read it. I don't go by that now though. Most people don't believe in it now. They just joke about it.

Says, "Do you plant it on the moon or do you plant it on the earth?"

Grandpa Cross died before I was born. He was born June 12, 1830 and died May 26, 1906. So I never knew him.

I never knew Grandma Cross either. I don't remember ever seeing her. She died—I must have been about four years old. I don't remember whether she was sick for any length of time before she died or how. Not too much would stay in my mind at that time. I can remember Mama, Julie, Lela, and Virgie going to the funeral, but I don't remember ever seeing Grandma. She was born October 4, 1837, and died November 19, 1914.

They are both buried in the Lick Creek Baptist Church Cemetery. Grandpa Cross was a Civil War Veteran; his grave has the Confederate marker.

Mama's parents, Francis and Alexander Taylor, were the grandparents I knew. Everybody called Grandma Taylor, Fanny, and Grandpa Taylor, Alex.

They lived right at the top of the road that went down and crossed Cabin Creek. The crossing was a ford, a shallow place in the water where wagons could drive across.

That's where Mama grew up. Their house was maybe a half hour walk from ours.

Mama was the oldest of seven children. She had three brothers, John, James and Zeb and three sisters, Freda, Mae and Bessie. Bessie and my sister Julie were near the same age; Irvin and Zeb were close in age too.

James died when he was little. James loved watermelon so good; he was eating watermelon and got a seed stuck in his windpipe. It swelled up and choked him to death. There wasn't nothing anybody could do to get it out. He wasn't more than just a tot. If he had been older someone could a-popped it out.

I wasn't around John and Zeb, enough to get to know them much. John went to California during the gold rush and lived out there. Zeb, he worked on the railroad on bridges and things like that.

Freda and Mae, and their families all lived down around where we did while I was growing up, so I got to know them.

Aunt Freda married Will Jarvis. They lived in a house right at the foot of High Rock Mountain. When I was older, they moved to Lexington.

Aunt Mae married Burt Greer and they lived, maybe fifteen

34

miles away, in Silver Hill. They bought a farm there and lived out their lives there.

Aunt Bessie was still at home. She married when I was about ten or eleven.


Aunt Mae and Uncle Burt had five children. Their ages run like stair steps, two years, maybe farther, apart. From time to time they'd come from Silver Hill in their horse-drawn wagon to visit and spend the night. We loved to see them come.

For entertainment, us kids we'd play games or climb trees in the woods. We never did have any toys to play with. We played with what we had and we did have a lot of trees. I could climb a tree as good as the boys.

Sometimes we'd play *ante-over*. That's the game where you divide up sides, then take a ball and part of us go on one side of the house and part on the other. Then someone throwed the ball over the house.

You had to catch it when it came over, or if you didn't catch it, you had to find it and throw it back. If the house was too tall we'd use an out building. We used our imagination.

At night Mama would put us in the beds crossways, one this way and one that. It was fun for us.


Grandpa Taylor had a good-sized farm with a big barn. He kept two or three horses or mules to farm with, and of course he kept cows for milk and butter. Everybody kept cows. He had a couple big fields he tended and he always had a pretty good size vegetable garden.

Grandpa raised corn for animal feed. When he harvested his corn, he would shock it up, and as he needed it he'd run it through his corn cutter. The corn cutter would cut it into little pieces so the animals could chew it.

We liked to walk to Grandma and Grandpa's and visit. Me and Frances and Fred would walk and dally along the way. We'd go for the day or maybe just go there and back for somethin' nother.

Near their house some gullies had washed out and red dirt had washed down them. The gullies were probably from where they had mined gold.

There used to be an old gold mine up on a hill between Cabin Creek and Bald Mountain. It was built a long time ago, sometime in the 1800s. It wasn't really much of a mine. They just dug the caves out by hand. They would dig some, then put up timbers to hold it up. They did get some gold from it though, but I never heard how much. It must have just give out after a while, 'cause it had already fell in when we lived there.

That's where Daddy's cousin, John, found his piece of gold. John came visiting, and one day he was down there walking around where the gold mine was and he found a piece of gold big as a quarter. I don't know what he ever did with it. Mama and Daddy never did say. There was gold there if they had-a-dug for it. I doubt if anybody would know where it is now except people that live down there.

We loved to play on the gullies around the old mines. Some of them were about as deep as a house. Some had old rotted timbers laying around with worms in them. The worms would make a *creechy, creechy, creechy* sound of grinding or sawing inside the logs.

Mama didn't want us playing around the gullies. I reckon she was afraid we'd get hurt or get dirty or something—that red dirt was terrible—so she told us the worms would come out and get us. She made the worms sound like monsters or something. She made us afraid to stop and play.

I spent a lot of nights with Grandma and Grandpa Taylor. Us kids would take turns. Sometimes one would go and sometimes two. Aunt Bessie was still at home then. She played the guitar for us, and she'd take us and play games with us and all.

I liked it most when I got to spend the night all by myself. Grandma had steps that went up into the attic. She had a bed up there and that's where I'd sleep. I liked that. Some of them were afraid to go up there, Frances didn't like to go up there, but it was always interesting to me. That's the difference in them and me I guess.

Grandma's kitchen always smelled good. She was always cooking somethin' nother and giving us something to eat. Sometimes she'd have a chicken killed and be cooking it and give us some of that, or she'd give us a ham biscuit or sausage biscuit or somethin' nother. I liked that. She had a heating closet on top of her stove and she always had meat up there to keep warm.

Her woodstove was different from Mama's. Hers had a water tank on the side to heat water. That was unusual for that time. 'Course she had to bring the water in and pour it into the heating tank. While she was cooking she'd lift up the lid and dip out the hot water with a dipper to put in her vegetables or what ever she wanted to use it on.

In the summer, Grandma's yard would be planted in the ole timey flowers, like bachelor buttons, marigolds and zinnias. Her geese and chickens and ducks would be roaming around all over. We loved to watch them.

Grandpa had a granary and smoke house, and we'd get to play around them. We'd get to do things we didn't get to do at home. I felt real special.

Grandma Taylor's daddy, my great grandpa, went off to the Civil War. He was a Bean, Sandy Bean. Grandma said she could remember seeing her daddy and mama hug and kiss one another and telling each other good-bye. Then she watched him leave and waved to him until he was out of sight. He never did come back. They never heard any more from him. I guess, after some years had passed, they pronounced him dead or something; anyway, she remarried to a Davis man and had children by him.

Grandpa Taylor had one brother that I know of. I think he was older than Grandpa. I don't know about sisters or anything, but his brother they called Monk. I don't know if that was his real name or why they called him Monk, but he was a talker. He was going on all the time. Every time they had a trial in Lexington he would bum a ride to town so he could be on the jury; I think you could volunteer back then.

⁂

Us kids were close, but Frances and Fred and me were *real* close. We would get out playing, and Frances was always a little bit—I reckon her knees or something wouldn't work just right. She was all the time falling down and she was all the time getting sick. If we would be playing and she would get hurt Fred and me would get a whipping, but we didn't hold no hard feelings.

They never had her to a doctor, so I don't know what was wrong. Her legs were always a bit stiff. She never liked to play like the rest of us, so I don't know what it was. Nobody else ever noticed it but Fred and me.

We run wild out in the woods, over the old Reid farm, across Cabin Creek and up the side of Bald Mountain. We roamed around all over those hills. We picked strawberries, blackberries and muscadines; sometimes blueberries if we could find them.

We searched for bullfrogs and sometimes we'd catch a pretty good-sized one. We caught them with our hands. We'd drive them under the rocks and watch where they went, and sometimes we'd see them sitting on the bank and catch them before they jumped. We did pretty good. We'd take them and clean them and Mama would fry them. If we'd find a turtle, why, we'd kill that. I don't know who did the cleaning of it, but anyway Mama would cook that and make turtle soup.

When people cleaned off new ground, they'd pile the brush up in the field and birds would come and roost in the brush pile. Then when they got ready to burn the brush, they'd burn of a-night while it was damp and the wind wasn't blowing.

When they set the brush on fire the birds would come flying out of the pile. We'd be standing around, ready with a piece of brush or somethin' nother, to knock them down. Then we'd catch them, clean them little birds and eat them. Some of them, you know, a sparrow, wouldn't have nothing much on it to eat, but we would eat them; we would eat everything edible I reckon.


In the summer we raised beans—green beans and dried beans. Mama left the dried beans in the shell and used on them all winter—what the bugs didn't get to. If she did shell any, she'd put those in jars, they'd save better that way.

Mama would pick the green beans, string them—I think she snapped them too—then she'd put them out in the sun and dry them like drying apples. When we got ready to eat them she'd just put them in water and let them soak and they'd be green again. They stayed good all winter. Now they're drying tomatoes like that, but we never did. We always canned tomatoes. We dried apples and peaches though. That was about the only fruit we had except blackberries and wild strawberries. Mama would make preserves out of the blackberries—the strawberries too if we happened to find enough.

We raised our own potatoes—sweet and Irish, and they are hard work. Daddy raised peanuts, just enough to eat, and we picked greens in the wintertime.

Food like coffee, salt, sugar, rice, things like that, Daddy bought at the general store in Newsom.

He took wheat and corn to the gristmill at Jackson Hill once every two weeks or so, depending on how much he took at a time, to be ground into flour and cornmeal, or he would just trade it.

We always kept a cow for milk, and Mama churned the cream for butter. She'd mold it or just roll it up in a ball with her hands and put it in a bowl for us to eat, not even molded. It was just as good that way.

To keep milk fresh, sometime we'd dig a hole in the ground, put a box in it, then set the milk down in the box. It kept the milk at ground temperature. That's all it would do.

Sometimes, if we lived close enough to a stream, we put the milk in crocks and set them in the stream to keep the milk cool. We'd just set it down in the water and fix it so the water wouldn't come up over the top. Then rocks or somethin' nother were used to hold the top in place so it would be clean; sometimes they'd just put a cloth over it. It was very risky.

When I was older we lived in a house that had a well right close to our back door. Mama, she'd put the milk in jars, put it in the well bucket, and let it down in the water to keep it cool 'til she got ready to use it. But, it would be too bad if somebody wanted to draw water.

The iron windlass that was used to crank the bucket up would get freezing cold in the wintertime. If you went out to draw water without gloves on, and if there was any moisture on your hands, they would stick to it. It would take the skin right off. It hurt! It was rough!

They'd say, "Go stick your tongue on it."

Some of us was dumb enough to do that. I never did.

# 6

Every year in the spring, Daddy would buy a couple pigs to fatten until fall to make enough meat to last us all winter, but sometimes it wouldn't last. He'd kill the pigs and salt the meat down; he salted the sides the hams and the shoulders.

It had to be cold weather to kill pigs, between 35 and 50 degrees. Daddy always killed around Thanksgiving. But sometimes it would still be too warm to kill, and if you did, you'd lose it. The meat wouldn't take the salt and it would spoil. It took at least three straight weeks of cold weather for the meat to cure.

Daddy saved most every part on the pig and Mama used it in some way. She'd take the fat and make lard out of it; that was our grease. She used the grease to make bread and gravy and to season food and things like that.

If Mama fried any meat she would always save the grease. She'd put it in a jar and use that grease first before she used the lard. If she didn't, it would get strong.

To make lard Mama took the left over fat and she cut it up into blocks and put it in a great big wash pot, if the skin was there she used that too. She built a fire under it and cooked 'em out. It would take a couple hours to cook 'em out. She cooked it 'til the cracklings began to get hard. The cracklings are the skins or meat after the lard is all cooked out of it. That's what they call the cracklings.

Mama put the lard in tin cans and closed it up tight. It would keep all winter long that way without getting strong. She took the cracklings, sealed them up as good as she could, and used on them 'til they run out. She would take a handful of cracklings and put them in cornbread. Boy, that was good!

I can eat cracklings all by their self; they sort of taste like the pigskins that you buy now, or like the fat on bacon. It was real good.

The jowls, the flesh under the lower jaw of the pig, most of the time Mama would slice that up, cook it and we'd eat it. Sometimes she would put it in salt and let it cure out. She'd take the kidneys, the liver and the lights, we called it the lights instead of the lungs, and she'd always fry that. Or sometimes she'd take the liver and make liver pudding, or liver mush which ever you want to call it. Then she'd take the feet and the bony part and the skinny part around the jowls and any other parts, cook 'em up all together, and make souse meat. It was a little bit sour. We loved that. Sometime I buy it yet, but it's got so much fat in it.

44

Mama scalded the tongue, scraped it off, cut it in strips or slices and boiled it. Sometimes she boiled it whole and then cut it in slices after she boiled it.

She'd take the entrails, the guts, and cut them in lengths about a yard long. She would clean all that stuff out and scrap them. Then turn them wrong side out, scald them, scrap them again, and then wash them good. After they were clean, she'd soak them in salt water and that's what we stuffed our sausage in. Even the stomach, some people empty that out and do it the same way. They called that the chitterlings. Mama didn't ever do that.

To make sausage Mama used the lean part of the scraps—scraps Daddy trimmed out from different places. Sometimes he would cut out some lean when he was trimming out the bacon or shoulder or the hams, like if he cut off a lean strip of the bacon when he trimmed it up to make it look better. And she'd also use the lean that was trimmed out around the jowls. She'd take all that to make sausage.

After she got her scraps all together, she'd put them through a meat grinder. Most everybody had a hand crank grinder that fastened to a table. When you grind sausage, you have to put some fat in too. If you don't put some fat in it, it won't grind up right. Most people like a whole lot of fat. After the sausage was ground, Mama stuffed it in the cleaned entrails.

There wasn't much about a pig that wasn't eat.

Everybody had a little log building with a chimney called the smoke house. We'd build a little fire in there with hickory wood

45

and it would give off a good smoke.

Then we'd take our salt cured meat and sausages and hang them in the smoke house to cure out with the smoke. We'd wrap the sausages around a pole, and hang them across ceiling rafters. Sometimes they would hang a whole side of meat up to cure out like that. The meat would absorb that smoke smell.

After it was cured, they put the smoked meat into flour-sacks or gunnysacks to keep the flies and insects away, and then it was hung in a cool dry place. It would last for months.

Everything was cured out or cooked so it would save. The liver pudding and souse meat, if it was kept cool, would last a long time. It would last until it got warm in the spring. You couldn't keep it after it got warm. We didn't have to worry about that though. We never had enough to last that long. We always had it eat up.

It was a lot of work, but it give us a lot of good things to eat.


We didn't kill cows. We kept them for milk and butter. When Daddy wanted to get rid of a cow, he would sell it or trade it off.

There were people that did kill cows. Sometimes somebody would kill one, and if it was cold enough, they would put it on a wagon, take it around to the people and sell it. That was the only way we had to get meat like that.


Mama raised the big Rhode Island Red hens. In the spring when it was time for the hens to start nesting she would always set the eggs and raise two or three bunches of chicks. When they'd get frying size, man we could live high.

To set the eggs, Mama would watch the eggs for fertility and save out the best ones. Mostly she just looked them over to see whether they looked like they would be good or not and so on. Now, they candle eggs for fertility by holding them up to a bright light to check for freshness. Mama didn't know about that then.

When it was the right time she'd put about ten or twelve eggs under a setting hen. The Rhode Island Reds were big and could cover a whole lot of eggs.

You had to watch the hens because sometime they would go to nesting on their own. They would hide their nest outside the chicken house and you couldn't find it. If that happened, you just had to wait and let them hatch their chicks out and then come up with their brood of little ones. You didn't get as many biddies that way.

Mama knew when the hens were ready to set, because they would quit laying and get *broody*, as we called it, and they would start clucking. That's the sound they'd make when they were nesting. They would sit on their nest all day except long enough to go get something to eat and drink, and they would go "cluck, cluck, cluck." That's when Mama would put the eggs she picked out in their nest.

They would sit on the eggs three weeks to hatch them. The hen would keep the eggs warm and turn them every day so they would hatch right. She would stick her head under her feathers and turn every egg every day. I don't know how she knew which ones to turn, but she kept them turned. It's very interesting to watch. But, sometimes, even with all that, they don't all hatch.

Daddy killed small wildlife, like rabbits and squirrels, for us to eat. He had a gun that he would shoot rabbits with. Everybody had a gun. Nobody knows what ever happened to Daddy's gun now.

He set gums in the woods around our house to catch squirrels and rabbits. The gums were rectangular wooden boxes a couple foot long, and six or eight inches wide with a trap door fixed so it would close when the animal went in to get the bait. He was real careful getting it out when he caught a squirrel, 'cause they would bite.

Rabbit meat was good. Mama always boiled them. A squirrel wasn't much meat. Sometime he'd catch a possum. He'd always save the possums for a month or so and feed them to fatten them up first. When Daddy killed possums he'd either scald or singe them to get all that old stuff off of them, then he'd clean them out. Mama fixed them about like any other meat. Possum was meat if you didn't have any other.

Mama did a lot of cooking on the fire in the fireplace. She had an oven pan that had legs on it that she used to cook with. If she wanted to make cornbread or somethin' nother, she would grease the bottom of it, put her food in it, and set the lid on top. Then she'd shovel a good many coals out from the fire, rake them out to the edge and set the pan on them. The lid had a lip that turned up about half and inch to hold coals. She would shovel coals on top of the lid and cook like that. That made some of the best cornbread I ever ate.

Fireplaces were a lot bigger back then and they had hooks in them that swung out to hold pots to cook with. Mama used pots some. Most of her pots were rounded on the bottom and had little legs on them so when she took them off the fire she could set them down. She'd put her meat or her vegetables in the pots, hang them on a hook and swing them around so they would be near the flame where it was hot so it would cook. After it had cooked some she could swing them out away from the flames where it was cooler. She could control the heat just a little bit like that. With the oven pan, she just used fire coals. Fire coals was all that controlled that, but bread would be done 'til those fire coals give out.

Sometimes Mama would use the oven pan to make the pone bread. It wasn't light bread, just biscuit bread. I guess she probably put meat in there too sometimes, I don't know. But I do remember the cornbread. When we were going to have milk and cornbread for supper, why, that pan would come out and Mama would make big ole hunks of cornbread. It was cooked all the way through— well, I'd say just right. It was real good.

Mama liked to bake cakes. She was always making cakes and pies. She would stir up the dough and make little sweet fried cakes like little pancakes. It was just fried bread. It was good. Everything she cooked I thought was good. 'Course I wasn't picky with my end.

For breakfast Mama would fix eggs if the chickens were

laying. If they weren't, she'd make gravy and we would have some kind of fruit if we had it. Sometimes when we had molasses, we'd take a clump of butter and put it in the molasses and rub it all together, and it would be caramel like. Or, we'd take the grease from fried ham or sausage and put that in the molasses. It made it good.

Table leftovers were put in a cool place or just covered and left on the table for the next meal. We tried to keep food as cool as we could, but that's all we had. If we had food left 'til the next day we'd most always re-cook it, but I don't know whether that killed the germs or not. I don't think anybody got sick from it. We did have some stomach throwing up sometime. That was a summer thing. It must have been a type of salmonella. It wasn't a bad type.

# 7

Irvin was still working in Tennessee the year the flu was so bad and so many people were dying. In the place where Irvin was boarding he said it was so bad that they just set the food down at the door, and if you were able to get up and come to the door, well all right, but if you weren't, well you didn't get nothing. He felt sorry for some of them. So, he'd go in and wait on them. He got the flu, but he didn't have it too bad.

Some of us caught it that year too, but we didn't have it bad, it wasn't much more than a cold. Mama put us all three, Fred, Frances and me, in the same bed in the fire room. She called the doctor from Jackson Hill and he gave us some pills or somethin' nother. We got all right. We were tough.

The First World War was still going on and they started drafting boys into service, Irvin wasn't but sixteen or seventeen, something like that, but he had told them he was eighteen. So when they started drafting the boys, he came home for a little while.

Irvin bought Fred a bicycle. Fred wouldn't let us girls ride it. I never learned to ride a bicycle. I never learned to skate either. I don't remember of Irvin ever buying me anything.

At that time, Julie was dating a boy. I don't remember just how old she was, but she was a-dating a boy. Irvin, he didn't like that boy at all. My Uncle Zeb, mama's youngest brother, and Irvin run around together, so one night Zeb and Irvin, they made a plan. They took some cans and tied strings in them and I don't know how they fixed them, but whatever they did, when they pulled on them it made a "squeak."

So, they went and hid around behind the house and when they heard Julie's boyfriend coming they begin to pull on the strings and they made this awful squeaking sound. That poor fellar like to broke his neck running. He never did come back. Julie just laughed. She didn't care anything about him. She laughed because they pulled that good trick on him.

When Zeb got a little older, he married a woman—I don't know her name—but she got sick and died. After she died he got to drinking.

Some years later, Zeb married again to a woman called Nellie. They had two children, a boy and a girl.

Julie and Bessie made friends with two girls at school. They were supposed to be well-to-do. Everything at their house was supposed to be spic and span and all. We did have a few well-off families around our community. Some of the richer ones had nice homes and a maid to help them. At school, boy, they'd stick their noses up to us like they were queens. It's always been that way. Classes of people.

Julie and Bessie invited these two girls to come to our house to spend the night. After they spent the night, us kids got to scratching our head and scratching our head and scratching our head, and Mama didn't know what was the matter.

She got to looking and looking and somebody ask, "What we looking for—lice?"

We had a head full of lice from those girls. Mama didn't know what to do. So she washed our hair in kerosene. It's a wonder it hadn't a cooked our brain, but that was the only thing she knowed to do. Sometimes they would put sulfur on the head for lice, but that would smell bad for a long time.

The kerosene did kill the lice. But after you killed the lice, if you wasn't careful and didn't kill the nits, the little eggs, they would come back and you'd be full of lice again. That's why it's so hard to get rid of them. They'd even get in the beds and on the clothes like bedbugs. We had bedbugs too.

Bedbugs are little, about like a tick, but soft not hard like a tick. Bedbugs bite and we would be red all over. Bedbugs are just as hard to get rid of as lice—maybe harder. They get everywhere, they even crawl into the walls. Mama would take the beds down and pour boiling water all over them. Then she'd put them outside, let them dry and put them back up. But that didn't get rid of them. They'd just scatter and crawl into the cracks of the walls.

Then something came out that would kill them. I don't remember the name of it, but it was used to kill bugs in the fields too. They made people quit using it after a while because it was found to be dangerous. It would kill the bedbugs though. It's a wonder it hadn't a killed us. We painted the whole house with it. Daddy put it in a bucket and just put it on the walls like paint. It would go in the cracks and kill the bedbugs. Then you could go to bed and go to sleep without worrying. We had to be tough.

There wasn't any electricity in the rural area where we lived. We used oil lamps for light at night. Mama didn't use candles. She was afraid of fire. Candles weren't safe. Fire was always a concern, even with oil lamps. The kerosene we used was stronger than what it is now. I don't know what the difference was, but if you didn't get the lamp trimmed just right sometimes it would catch a-fire.

When we was living on the other side of the mountain where the back door opened off the kitchen at ground level and then just kept going up the hill, one night the lamp flared up. Mama ran to the door with it and throwed it out up the hill. It rolled back down against the house, but it went out before it caught the house a-fire.

Sometimes a lamp would explode, and sometimes someone would turn them over and catch a house on fire, but we never did have a fire.

We very seldom ever had more than one lamp lit to a room.

We had large lamps for the kitchen to give light to work by and eat by and smaller ones that we used for the bedrooms. Some people had lamps that sat on a little thing that fastened on the wall. Some people had the fancy ones. Mama got one of the fancy ones one time, but she didn't use it much. It cost too much to burn.

We had to trim the lamps and clean the chimneys every day. That was a daily task. The smoke from the blaze smokes up the glass chimney and if you don't clean it, it want give off light. Then the wicks burn, sometimes more on one side than it does the other. We had to trim them and be sure to refill the lamps every evening so they had plenty of oil in them of a-night. If we ran out, it was just too bad. We'd have to sit by the fireplace to see.

We had some smaller lamps, about three inches tall, that looked a little like a candle. They didn't have a chimney. The oil basing was round and flat on the bottom and had a handle like a teacup. They used these little lamps to quilt by. They would set it right on the quilt and just push it along as they worked.

Of course we had the lanterns; we used them for outside—if we went out of a-night. At night if the adults needed to use the toilet they usually took the path—if they weren't afraid. Lots of them were afraid of animals being around. There were no humans around to bother them, nothing like that. The houses were far apart. It might be miles before anybody else was around. Doors was never locked. Robbery? Never, except sometimes if somebody got hungry they'd open up the smoke house and get a ham or shoulder or what ever they could find.

The women made quilts in their spare time. They enjoyed gathering at somebody's house to visit and sit and quilt. Mama and Grandma Taylor made quilts together. To start a quilt, they took bundles of cotton and carded them down. To card it, they'd take a whip or a small stick or somethin' nother and whip the cotton down. There would be cotton flying all through the air. They whipped it until the cotton stretched out flat.

Then, they'd spread the cotton on top of a quilt bottom they'd made from large pieces of scrap cloth—usually flour or feed sacks sewed together to the size of a bed. On top of that they spread the quilt top—made of small pieces of cloth that were sewed together in squares of some kind of pretty design. Sometimes in a pattern like a fan or star, or some other design, or it could just be pieces of scrap cloth sewed together at random.

After the layers were put together, they attached the quilt to a quilting frame made of four long poles, two poles placed on opposite edges of the quilt. Thumbtacks or something like that were used to fasten the edges to a pole on each side then the other poles was sandwiched on top of those and fastened tightly together with pegs. This was to hold the quilt in place while it was being quilted.

Some quilting frames had hooks fastened to the ceiling with pulleys so the frame could be raised up to the ceiling when they weren't working on it and let back down when they were ready to quilt again. But most of the time, women just used four ladder back chairs. They'd set the chairs in a square and place the frame on the back of each chair with the quilt spread out between them.

Sometimes several women would come to one house to work on a quilt, or maybe it would be two women in the same house, a woman and her daughter. That's all they had to do in the wintertime. They couldn't get out nowhere, so they'd do that.

Before they sat down to quilt, they'd collect everything they needed and lay it out on the quilt. Everything would be sitting right there in front of them, their needles and thread and scissors, and if it was night, a little quilting lamp to see by; they didn't have to get up for nothing. When everything was ready, they'd get around the quilt in their chairs and dip snuff and quilt.

About all the women, and some of the men, dipped snuff back then. Daddy didn't dip, but he raised a little tobacco that he chewed on. He'd just chew on the dried leaves after it was cured.

The women used a twig toothbrush to dip with. They'd get a twig of sweet gum not as big around as my little finger and about four or five inches long. They'd skin it back a little bit and chew on it 'til it was a soft brush. Then they'd dip it in the snuff and hold it in their mouth and chew on it. They'd sit there with their toothbrush in their mouth and quilt and talk.

After they quilted the edges in about as far as they could reach, they'd roll it up and quilt on the inside. They didn't have to roll up the ends, just the sides where the quilt was attached to the poles.

When they were finished quilting for the night they'd roll it up and put it out of the way, and then put it back out to work on the next day.

They made some beautiful things. Most women were pretty good quilters. Some made short stitches and some long. The short stitches were the best. Some quilted straight, some in designs like flowers or fans. Some made their own designs. That gets fancy. I had some pretty quilts that Mama made, but they wore out.

Tacking is another way of making a quilt. Instead of sewing the layers together with a quilting stitch, they'd tack or tie the layers together. Tacking is easier and faster than quilting. Tacking is where you take strong thread or yarn and sew down through the quilt, then bring it back up and tie a hard knot. The thread is cut off about a half-inch long. It's tied like that every few inches and won't come out. Tacking wasn't as pretty as the quilting unless there was a design for it.

Some women made their own thread. Grandma Taylor had a big spinning wheel that she made thread on. She'd take cotton, card it out and roll it up. Then she would start it off in the spindle and it would come off in thread. Mama didn't learn how to use it too well. I don't know what ever went with Grandma's spinning wheel.

# 8

Daddy raised cotton. We picked it in the fall; all us kids helped. He paid other people to come and help us, but it wasn't much.

The adults wore long cotton picking bags that had a strap that went over their shoulder. They dragged the bags along behind them as they picked. As the bag got full it would get heavy. Some had longer bags than others.

Us children, we picked in something like a big tow-bag. Daddy took the corners of the bag at the top and brought them together and tied a knot; then he'd put it around our neck. Boy, we would be so tickled when we got a bag full.

After the picking was over Daddy piled the cotton in his wagon to take to the gin in Lexington. Taking the cotton to the gin and returning home was a two day trip. Sometimes he let me go with him. Sometimes Mama would go with him and leave us children home to cook and take care of ourselves, and me just ten years old or younger.

Daddy's wagon was an open bed, with big high side planks. There was a seat in front that two people could sit on—just a board, no cushion unless you took one.

He'd pile all the loose cotton in the wagon first, he'd pile it high; then he'd put some of the tow-bags of cotton on top and tie it all down to keep everything in. He could haul—I think 'til he got a whole load—it would make a bale.

Daddy's two mare workhorses, Maude and Nell, pulled the wagonload of cotton to the gin. They were pretty horses—mostly white with a little gray. They were gentle. They never pushed us away when we'd go up to them. They'd let us get on them and ride and go all around them and play with them and never kick or anything like that. Both of them were getting on in age, but they were strong. They were good workhorses.

When Daddy let me go to the gin with him, we'd leave home at daylight and drive the horses a steady pace up Highway 8 all the way to Lexington. The trees would be turning, the frogs would be hollering and sometime we'd see a rabbit. Daddy would tell me tales all the way, things of his childhood and stories. You can imagine how exciting it was to get to go if you hadn't never been anywhere.

As the morning passed, we drove by High Rock, Healing Spring, Lick Creek and usually got to Southmont 'til lunchtime. There was a store to the left on the north side of the Yadkin River bridge, I believe Peacocks run it then. On the right side there was a place with some trees and a water pump. Daddy would pull the wagon in there and water and feed the horses. After they were taken care of, if we hadn't brought anything from home, he'd go in the store and get us something to eat, a can of sardines or some crackers and cheese or somethin' nother. We'd eat, and then we'd drive on in to Lexington.

It would be dark 'til we come up over the last hill into town. When we topped the last hill, we could see the lights from town. It was so pretty, it looked about like a fairy tale to me.

In Lexington, we spent the night with Daddy's nephew Lee Cross and his wife Nannie. Lee's wife's name was Nancy, but she was called Nannie like Mama.

Peter Lee and Nancy Marie Hulin Cross

Lee was younger than Daddy, but Daddy and Lee were close. They were closer than any of my other cousins were that I knew of.

Lee was Daddy's oldest brother Jim's son by an earlier marriage; Jim was quite a bit older than Daddy. His first wife,

Rebecca, Lee's mother, died sometime along the way and Jim remarried to a woman called Nell.

Lee lived on West 10<sup>th</sup> Avenue in a Wenona cotton mill house. Nannie worked at the Wenona. Their house was a small two story with two bedrooms, three by using the living room part as a bedroom too. It was crowded.

Lee and Nannie had a gob of kids, fourteen or fifteen in all including a set of twins, a boy and a girl, but at that time, they only had five or six. The oldest girl, Blanche, wasn't quite as old as me.

Lee worked for the Lexington Bakery in the baking part. He worked there for years. When he quit he was the manager.

That night I slept with the girls. Early the next morning Daddy took the cotton to the gin. Then we started for home. The ride home was as good as the ride to town.

Many of the communities we passed through had churches with the same name as the community; like Cotton Grove Methodist Church and the community of Cotton Grove had the same name and Lick Creek Baptist Church and the community of Lick Creek had the same name and Jackson Hill Methodist and Jackson Hill had the same name. Most all of the communities had a post office and a store, some had a place where the southbound train stopped to pick up passengers. And every community had their doctor.

The Cotton Grove store on Highway 8 had a Southbound train stop, but they didn't sell the tickets there because it wasn't a regular stop. If someone wanted to get on the train, the station keeper would flag the train down; they had the signals. The train also stopped there to pick up mail and so on.

I remember one time, I must have been about seven years old, Mama, Daddy, me, Frances and Fred caught the Southbound train at High Rock and rode it to the Cotton Grove Store. We got off the train there and walked the rest of the way, maybe five miles, to Linwood to visit Daddy's cousin Frank Alley. One of Daddy's sister's had married an Alley—Frank's daddy—so Frank was Daddy's cousin.

I can remember the walk well. Fred was too small to do much walking so we had to carry him. On the way, we stopped to rest at a colored couple's house and they gave us some water out of an oak water bucket. That was the best water out of that oak bucket, it was so good and cold.

The woman was making baskets. I was very much interested in the basket making as little as I was. That was something to see.

We spent the night with Daddy's cousin Frank and the next day we walked to the Southern train stop in Linwood and rode the Southern to the depot in uptown Lexington.

Families were waiting at the depot to be picked up by relatives. Relatives would come in buggies or surreys to pick them up—sometimes even a car—not many people had cars back then. We didn't have anybody to pick us up; we walked the couple miles from the depot to Lee's house. We most always walked from the Southbound or the Southern depots to wherever we were going.

Sam Billings was the first to run taxis from the depots. I would say it was in the late teens or early twenties. He'd pick people up and take them wherever they wanted to go.

Sam's taxis could carry a lot of people; they were the bigger makes of cars. He might have had Cadillac's—it was one of those big cars.

The old abandoned Lexington Southbound Railroad Depot.
Located off West 5th Avenue on Southbound Street near the railroad bridge.
The depot burned down in the early 2000s, not long after this photo was taken.

I got to ride in the taxis once or twice as a small child, but always with somebody else and didn't pay any attention to what it cost to ride.

Some time during the depression, I don't remember exactly when, the taxi company sold out. Later on, Sam started and ran the Billings Trucking Co.

At High Rock, below where the High Rock dam is now and

on the other side of the railroad, there was a little stream with a bridge across it. It was like a little island in there. People used it like a beach or vacation place. They built up concession stands in there, sold homemade ice cream and cakes and things like that. I can remember the homemade strawberry ice cream being so good.

People would come down there from Lexington on the Southbound passenger train to spend the day. People from all around the area would come. Sawmill workers would come in there too—I reckon just to blow off. People came across the Yadkin River from the Rowan County side on the Bringle Ferry to spend the day.

The ferry was just a short ways below where the High Rock dam is now. There was no dam there then. It was just the Yadkin River at High Rock.

The Bringle Ferry took passengers from the Davidson County side of the Yadkin River to the Rowan County side or vice versa. It was big enough to carry a couple wagons with horses. The ferry was fastened with chains to a cable or trolley line that ran across the water. When someone needed it and it was on the other side, they'd holler for it. The ferry operator would take long poles and pole it across the river and get whoever was waiting and take them to the other side. When they got to the other side, if anybody was waiting they would do the same. They would go backwards and forwards by pushing the long poles down to the bottom of the river and pushing the ferry along. They didn't have electricity or motors then.

Wagons paid a fee to go across, but us children could go

down there and if we wanted to see somebody on the other side they would just say, "Come on and get in." We never had to pay.

When the river water got up high during a rain, the ferry couldn't go across because the poles weren't long enough to reach to push it along. Or if the river got too swift, they couldn't go across.

They never had much trouble with the ferry, but when they did need to make repairs, they had a ladder that they used to go up to the trolley line to work on it.

# 9

Mama thought she wasn't going to have any more babies after Fred, and then they come double. When Cora and Flora were born I didn't really know what was going on, but I remember it. I guess I was about eight years old.

Cora was born first. She was born early in the day. Mama was upstairs with the granny woman, I could hear a baby crying and they said we had a new baby. We weren't allowed to go upstairs.

Mama had a rough time with Flora. She wasn't born 'til later on in the late evening. They finally had to get the doctor. The doctor didn't know much more than the granny woman did though. The doctors didn't know nothing back then. The granny woman delivered most of the babies and women got along just as good, unless it was a severe case. When it comes to a breech birth or something like that then they had their problems.

Mama didn't know she was having twins; it's a wonder she

lived. But the babies were both healthy.

While the twins were still small, the Reid's had a sawmill to come in and cut the timber off their land. They had a truck that they used to go in and haul the logs out with. But the hired workers had to come and go by wagon, so they couldn't get in and out to go home every day. Mama boarded some of them. They would stay with us for a week at a time.

While they were staying with us, Red Creek Church was having revival meetings. It seemed like an awful long ways to Red Creek Church, but it couldn't have been more than a few miles from where we lived. One night the sawmill workers all decided they wanted to go to the revival. So they took the sawmill truck and took the whole family. We all piled on the back of the truck.

Cora and Flora were about a year old. They might not a-been quite a year old. They were just little; they had to hold them in their arms.

To get to the meeting, we had to go by Grandma Taylor's house and cross Cabin Creek at the ford. Then we went on to the meeting.

We got to the meeting all right, but on the way home it rained. I never in my life, well I hadn't before that, remember it raining so hard.

When we got to Cabin Creek, the water had got up. The water had got up so fast 'til when the truck got in there, it couldn't get up the bank on other side. So we all had to get off the truck and walk up the bank in the pouring rain.

Oh that rain, and they were carrying the twins and all! We walked up the hill and on by Grandma Taylor's. Then we walked through the pouring rain over to our place. It was scary, but it was exciting too. We did have some exciting times.

Mama made wine for the sawmill workers. She would have us go out and pick blackberries or strawberries or whatever we could get. She made wine and she made *some* medicines. People back then knew about different homemade things that were used for medicines. Mama mostly made bark teas.

One tea she used, was sassafras tea. She broke off the tender twigs, boiled them and made tea. When she sweetened it, it was good. I read in a magazine that some used the roots to make the tea, but Mama was afraid or didn't know to use the roots. Her tea wasn't too strong that way. She gave it to us to build our body up, especially in the spring. Sassafras tea helps you get out of the winter drawls.

Mama used to make cherry bark cough syrup from wild cherry tree bark. She used catnip for baby's colic, rye plants to make a poultice for sores on our legs or feet. She used to make a poultice for boils—to draw it out, but I don't remember what it was. She went out and got bark and plants when she needed them to make different things.

She gave us castor oil or Epsom salts for a laxative and I hate both of them now. We treated infections with Vaseline or Cloverine salve. We'd soak the infection in warm salt water or boric acid water. That was supposed to draw out the infection and

69

kill the germs.

For something serious people went to the doctor—if they were able to go. If they weren't, the old country doctors, they'd come to the house. Back then he traveled either on a horse or in a buggy. Later on he'd have a car. But lots of roads, a car couldn't hardly go over. The old country doctors were more like nurses, you had emergency services and that was it. If you broke a bone, they would set it of a sort, but it was happy go lucky if it healed all right, if not it was just too bad. That was the way. A lot of babies died. It's a wonder anybody lived.

Mama never said anything about my baby brother that died at birth, except that he was born dead. I don't know what he died of, maybe he was a breech baby or something like that, I don't know.

The first death I really remember was a little boy that lived down at Healing Springs crossroads. I don't know what he had, but he was sick almost a year. He could have had cancer, could have had something else. Whatever he had the doctors didn't know how to treat him. I felt so sorry for him. That was the first I definitely remember about death.


Some believed in ghosts. Older men would get together and tell ghosts stories. They used to tell a story about the big tree at the end of the road that went between our barn and the pasture gate. It was said that a man riding a horse ran under a limb of the tree, caught his head and broke his neck and died. Some didn't like to go by that tree because they said the man's ghost was still around.

Some thought they might *see* a ghost. Some believed in it. But I never believed in it. It was just a tale to me.

I never was aware of being afraid or scared of anything. I didn't know what to be afraid of. I can remember one thing though.

A man lived by himself on the other side of Bald Mountain, and of a-night he would walk up the railroad to our house or either to Grandma and Grandpa Taylor's and he'd sit and talk. He'd talk sometimes 'til 10 or 11 o'clock it seemed like.

One night he left our house and started home by way of Grandpa Taylor's. He went on by Grandpa Taylor's and then went down toward the railroad. The Southbound went to the lower side there between Grandpa's farm and the river. When he got down to the railroad he saw something.

Well, he come a-running back up to Grandpa's, got him to the door and said with a frightened voice, "I saw a bear down there!"

So, everybody got the word around, and we put chairs and everything up against the doors thinking the bear would come and come in. Nobody knew anything much about bears. I wasn't afraid though. I guess I was more curious than anything else.

Well, all the men took their guns and went out a-hunting that bear. When they finally got down to the railroad, it was Grandpa's yearling calf had got out and was standing on the other side of the railroad. It was black and he thought it was a bear. I don't remember him coming back after that.

When I think about it, it's so funny how people can see things and imagine everything else.

# 10

In the fall when the corn was harvested, we had corn shuckings. We loved corn shuckings. We'd get to play and eat lots and lots of food. Wagons full of pulled corn would come in to the barnyard and unload, one wagon at a time. One would join where another left off and make a long row or circle of corn in the barnyard.

Then one night they would have a corn shucking. All the women would cook. They cooked chickens and pork and vegetables, and they'd bake cakes and pies, all kinds of stuff and bring it to the corn shucking.

Then everybody would get around the corn pile and shuck corn. They'd shuck 'til ten o'clock—if they could get it done 'til ten. Some used a peg to shuck with, some used gloves. If you didn't have a peg or gloves to shuck with, you shucked it with your fingers. A peg is a little piece of wood or metal with a strap that fits around the fingers with a kind of sharp point or peg on one end. You put the peg or point in the shuck, pull one way with the peg and pulled the other way with the other hand and the shuck would come apart. That way it didn't hurt your hands as much. If we wore gloves to shuck with, sometimes our hands would get sore even through the gloves.

After the ear of corn was shucked, we threw it over across the corn pile, or if it was a circle we threw it into the center.

Us children, boy, we were having a time. If girls and boys were dating or sitting close together and the boy found a red ear of corn he got to kiss the girl. That put excitement in it.

If the shucking wasn't finished 'til ten o'clock, they'd quit anyway and go to the house and wash their hands, then everybody went in and eat. That was the fun part.

The next day whoever's house the corn shucking was at, would get up the corn and put it in their corncrib.

We'd go to one house, like tonight, then maybe another house tomorrow night and somebody else's another night. It wasn't uncommon for those families that had come a long way to spend the night in the farmer's barnyard.


The wheat threshing was as much fun and exciting to us children as the corn shucking was.

Daddy harvested his wheat by hand with an old-timey reaper. First, he would take a cradle and go along and cut it. The cradle had long fingers attached to a scythe. He'd give it a cut and the wheat would just fall over on those fingers. He would drop the cut wheat aside into a pile and then make another cut. Two acres a day is about the average, when using a cradle to harvest wheat.

After it was cut, somebody, usually the women, came along behind and gathered the wheat and tied it in bunches. Then others would come along and shocked it. To shock it, they stood several of the bunches up together in a circle. Then they'd take two more bunches and bend them to make a little point to them and put them over the top so the rain water would run off. The shocks were left there in the field for maybe two months before they got there with the threshing machine to thresh it.

Us kids, we'd be out every day watching for the thresher to come. They pulled it with a steam engine and it would be putting out a big puff of smoke.

They'd blow their whistle and we'd holler, "Here they come! They coming! They coming!"

We were all excited.

When the thresher came, all the neighbors would come around with their wheat and all. They'd take their teams and wagons and haul their shocks of wheat to the threshing machine.

If you had a whole lot of wheat, sometimes it would take two days to thresh it. But we never had that much.

After the thresher was set up, some of the men would cut the bands on the bundles, and others would throw the bundles into the thresher. One person had to stand up high on the thresher to move the straw blower pipe. That's a big pipe that reaches a way up and throws the straw out after it's separated from the wheat. It blows it out onto a big pile.

When the threshed wheat comes out, somebody stands down

there and catches it and measures it by the bushel with a bushel basket. Then, however the land was rented, the wheat was divided. They would set the landowners wheat in one place and the renters in another. Most of the time the land owner had somebody there to make sure he got what he was supposed to get.

The girls were never allowed to help with the threshing. The men and the boys did that. The girls helped out at the house fixing food or tending to the children or getting in the wood and all that. We had a big time. That was a big thing when the thresher came. It was work, no doubt about it, but we had fun. We enjoyed it. We sung songs, but I don't remember them.

When wintertime came we looked forward to playing in the snow. I remember quite a few big snows. Some would get up to our waist. When I was staying at Aunt Ellen and Uncle Burl's, it snowed up to their knees, of course it was farther than that on me. They had to shovel a path about three hundred foot out to the spring to get water. I enjoyed it, but I don't know whether the adults enjoyed all that shoveling or not.

Mama always made snow cream. That was a real treat. She would make it with sugar, vanilla flavoring, cream and eggs. They don't put raw eggs in it now because of bacteria, but we did then.

It was fun to get in a snowball fight. On the way to school, the boys would throw snowballs at the girls. But if the snow was very deep or if it was snowing hard, Mama wouldn't let us go to school.

We didn't have sleds, but sometimes we'd take a dishpan or

somethin' nother and sit down in it and go down a little hill.

One time I got the idea that it would be fun to slide down one of Daddy's haystacks. The snow laying on top of it made it look nice and round and all. I didn't know at the time that under the snow, it had a layer of ice on it too.

I don't remember how I got up there, but I got up on top of it and sat down—ready to slide. Then, I give a little push. When I started to slide my weight broke the ice, and as I went down, the ice took the skin off my legs. That didn't feel so good. I think I was the only one dumb enough to try that.

Mama recognized our birthdays, but not every time. Sometime she'd make us a new dress—if she had money to get the material—or she might make us something to eat a little different from what we'd been a-having. Just little things. 'Course she didn't have a lot of extra time.

For Christmas, we'd have a little bit of celebration and so on, but there wasn't much we could do. We were so crowded up in the house that we didn't have room for a tree. One year Mama found some pretty holly and she cut that and put it in a bunch and hung it up to the ceiling and that was our Christmas tree. Virgie and Frances and me slept right under it in a foldout trundle bed.

At night we would sing, "Hang your stockings in a row Santa Clause comes tonight!"

I can remember that well.

I think that was the year I got my doll—the only doll I ever got from Mama and Daddy. It had that composition face, the kind that if it got wet, it peeled off.

I made a playhouse outside for my doll by putting sticks and rocks around and using this, that and the other. We had a good imagination. We used a rock or maybe a stump for the stove. We used big leaves or something like that for dishes; we'd cup them up and call them our bowls. Sometimes we took wild molly pops and got the seeds out of them and they made pretty dishes. They looked just like a dish. We put our play food in them. We didn't have anything real.

When the molly pops get yellow, they're good to eat. We'd eat the inside; you don't eat the outside. We just scooped it out. It tastes something like cantaloupe.

For dolls, sometimes we'd take, if it was in season, we'd take a small ear of corn that had the silks on it and shuck it and that would be our doll—the silks would be the dress.

One night I forgot and left my Christmas doll, the doll that Mama and Daddy gave me, outside in my playhouse. It rained and ruined it. After that, I had the body part, but the face all peeled off.

We got a little red wagon for Christmas one year. I guess it was for all of us, but Fred claimed it. One day we were all just playing around with it, riding it down a hill near our house. The hill was steep, steep enough to make the wagon go fast. A little ditch had washed out from the rain and some hand size rocks were laying around.

The wagon was small, only one could ride at a time, so we were taking turns. When it came my turn, I got in and got to going down the hill. The wagon got to going fast. Too fast. I couldn't keep it guided straight and it hit the ditch and knocked the front wheels around. Whap! Over I went. My knee hit a rock and cut it. Deep. When I got home Mama washed it with soap and water and bandaged it up. I still carry the scar.

# 11

I guess I was about eight or nine when we moved out from the
Reid farm. From there, we moved up near High Rock
Mountain to the Kinney house. Mr. Kinney was a mail carrier and
owned the farm. Daddy sharecropped for him. Mama's youngest
sister, Bessie, had married Bill Cole and they lived in the next
house over from us.

The Kinney house was a two story; two bedrooms upstairs
and two bedrooms downstairs, then the dining room and kitchen
all together—just an ordinary unpainted farmhouse.

We kept going to Fredonia School for a little while after we
moved. We walked down cross Cabin Creek—I don't know how
far through the woods—but it was a pretty good ways. We didn't
mind.

Then Mama decided to send us to Lick Creek School. Lick

Creek School was on the road between High Rock and Lick Creek Church. It was a pretty good ways to walk, but maybe not quite as far as Fredonia.

Lick Creek School was a one-room school with a potbelly stove. The boys sat on one side and girls on the other. The grades went from the first grade on up. Inside the front door was a small entrance room with shelves on either side. That's where we'd hang our coats and put our lunch, boy's stuff on one side and girl's on the other.

Sometime the boys would go out to be excused or something—or it could have been girls too—and they would get into your lunch and take it. We had all kinds.

We had to go out to the woods to be excused. The older ones would take the younger ones. We had to get somewhere we couldn't be seen. In the wintertime, it was hard to get to a place where you couldn't be seen—the leaves were all off the trees. That wasn't strange to us though. We were used to it.

The playground where we played was in front of the schoolhouse. We'd play ball or somethin' nother like that, but sometimes us girls, we'd go back behind the schoolhouse and make us a playhouse. Sometimes we'd get so interested in playing they'd have to send somebody to get us.

At Lick Creek School, my friends were my cousin Lillian Davis, the Rogers girls and the Will Cross girls; they weren't any kin to us. Those were my close friends.

Boy friends? There was one boy I liked, but as far as a friend, I don't know whether he liked me or not. He was one of the nicest.

He lived down near High Rock Mountain. Wilbur was his given name, but I can't think of his last name. His sister grew up to be a teacher.

My cousin Lillian and me sat in a desk together. You can imagine two girls sitting together. We'd get to talking and get to giggling about somethin' nother and they called us "giggles."

The teacher said, "I'm going to have to separate you all."

But, she never did.

I think Miss Skeen was our teacher then. There were three teachers at Lick Creek. One was a Snider man. Another was Miss Skeen. I can't remember the other one.

I always liked reading. I did fairly well with my arithmetic and I liked history. They didn't go into it deep with that many children all in different grades. They just had a few minutes of each class.

They'd take the ones up front who were doing their lessons. The others were supposed to be studying, but they'd be cutting up. The teacher would get on to them; they could spank them then. The bigger boys would give them a lot of trouble—tease the girls and all that—but they still managed them better than they do now.

We went to school six months out of the year, mostly in the wintertime. It was probably October when we started school, something like that. Some people raised cotton, and needed the children to help. It was warm when we got out in the spring, probably April or the first of May.

Before we moved to Lick Creek we didn't go to church 'cause we lived too far away. At Lick Creek, the Lick Baptist Church was within walking distance of our house, so we walked to church most every Sunday.

In the summer time when they'd have the revival meetings at Bakers Springs, it's called Summerville now, anyway, it was Baker Springs then, Daddy would take us in the wagon and we'd go to night service. It would be midnight 'til we got back home. We'd lay in that wagon, well I did, I don't know about the other children, they probably went to sleep, but I'd lay there and look up at the stars and wonder about them. It was beautiful.

When Julie and Lela were in their early teens, they left home and went to Lexington to work in the cotton mill. They'd let them work in the cotton mill at fourteen then, maybe younger than that. Lee and Nannie took them in as boarders.

Virgie stayed at home for a little while, but then she quit school and went to town too. She was no more than twelve or thirteen. At first, she stayed with Lee and Nannie working for them babysitting. Staying with Lee and Nannie was considered all right. They were in the family. Mama and Daddy didn't mind letting her go out like that.

When Virgie left I was the oldest one left at home.

Daddy managed to buy a buggy. I don't know how he managed it. He never had much money. Irvin was giving him some money and the girls that were working in town were giving him some, or he might have traded something for it, or both.

It was just a regular two seater one-horse buggy. The top was shaped like a baby carriage and was covered in a black canvas that had tar or something on it to keep it from leaking.

Daddy took us places in it. He'd take us to church on Sunday mornings. We'd all squeeze in, some holding others on their lap.

That fall when the wheat thresher came around we all piled in the buggy and went to the wheat threshing.

Aunt Mae and Aunt Freda were there.

Aunt Mae came up to Mama all excited, telling her how she'd left something she needed for the supper at home. I don't remember just what it was, but it was important to her to have it.

Aunt Mae says, "Well how in the world can I get it? The men are all busy with the wheat threshing."

Aunt Mae's house was about five miles or so from where we were.

"Well," somebody says, "Alma and Beulah can go get it. They can go in the buggy."

I wasn't no more than ten years old at the time and my cousin Beulah, Aunt Freda's girl, was the same age as Frances, about eight.

Daddy had showed me a little bit about driving the buggy; mostly the horse would just go by itself.

So, we agreed to go.

Aunt Mae says to me, "Now hurry up!"

So I did!

Beulah and me, we started out, and I run that mare half the way there. The buggy was just bouncing along. It's a wonder it hadn't a throwed us out. But we were able to stay in, and the horse stayed in the road so she didn't hit nothing.

Well, we got there, and we got whatever it was she forgot, and we got back all right, but I don't know why in the world they ever put us kids in that job. I would be afraid to put one of mine to doing something like that.

I never did tell nobody I run that horse like that.

Daddy finally traded the buggy for a surrey. It had a canvas top and was bigger, longer than the buggy. Some of the surreys was fancy and had a fringe all around the top. I don't remember for sure if Daddy's had a fringe, but every time I hear that song, *A Surrey with a Fringe on Top*, I think of Daddy's surrey.

The surrey could ride five comfortably, maybe six if they were small—the little ones sitting between. Daddy took us to church in it too, and sometimes he took us visiting.

Mama's younger sister, Aunt Bessie, died. She was pregnant with her second baby. She had her first baby all right. It was a girl. Then with her second baby she had a different doctor. He was from Denton. Bill's sister was pregnant at the same time and they both had that same doctor from Denton.

When time came for Bessie to have the baby, Bill's sister came and stayed with her to help. After the birth, Bessie had problems getting over it. She couldn't get well. She got worse and worse, and finally she died and left the baby.

Then that same doctor delivered Bill's sister's baby and she died the same way Bessie did. We all figured they took the infections because the doctor didn't take care of them right. He didn't know what he was doing. If they don't know what they are doing they can do a lot of damage. Bill took it real hard.

A woman from the Home Extension came around to the schoolhouse and give us a talk about starting the 4-H clubs. They didn't call it the 4-H Club then. Home Extension hadn't been organized very long and they didn't have nothing for the children yet, so they were trying to get something started.

She wanted us girls to learn how to make bread, and to make it on our own. So well, I was about 10 years old, something like that, so I go ahead, I sign up.

I had cooked some. One time Mama took Frances, Fred and the twins and went visiting for a couple days and left me at home to cook for Daddy. For breakfast I made biscuits, I could make biscuits, and I fixed some ham to go with them. I thought I was doing a good job, but when I went to fry the ham, I salted it and it was already salted. Poor ole Daddy ate it anyway.

The home extension woman gave us all the papers and

everything to show us how to make bread—the recipe and all how to do it. All the girls were supposed to make bread and take it to school. So I went ahead and made mine, and Mama didn't help me at all.

One of the girls was fifteen years old and she'd been cooking a long time. So everybody knew she would get first place. When the Home Extension agent examined everybody's biscuits, she picked my biscuits. And I got to come to Lexington to a countywide biscuit baking contest.

In Lexington one of my cousin Lee's daughters tried to help me make the bread. If I had been left alone I might have done something. I didn't even place in that one. 'Course, all over Davidson County, why that's to be expected. I wasn't that good a cook, but I was very proud.

One night, while we lived at the Kinney farm, I had a dream. In my dream there was a field and at the backside of it there was a straight road. The road went between part of the farm we lived on and part of a farm that joined us.

I dreamed I had a car and was driving along that straight road. I dreamed that I was going to Fredonia School and I imagined I could go by and pick up my friends and drive them to school.

Whatever that came from I don't know. I had big thoughts, a big imagination. The way I imagined the car, was something like a little doodlebug, just a little car that two of us could get in. I was imagining things that were in the future. Cars of the future. I have thought about that so much. I was a-seeing things.

When I get on a road that is long and straight I think about that. It just shows how your mind can travel around.

# 12

When I was about twelve years old we moved to Lexington. I was too young to remember all the details of why we moved, but if Daddy would have had the help, he could have done real good on the Kinney place. But Irvin was off again working doing pipefitting and 'til Fred came along big enough to help, Daddy was about give out. So we moved to Lexington in Daddy's horse-drawn wagon.

I hadn't been wishing or anything about living in Lexington. I had been to town, but I didn't know what anything was like living in town. Before we moved they were just beginning to talk about cutting out Lick Creek School and sending us to Denton to school. Mama didn't like that and that was another reason we moved.

We moved into a house on Salisbury Road near the Wenonah Cotton Mill. Grover Myers run a store right beside our house. He's dead now. It was a small unpainted one-story house—two bedrooms, a living room, a dining room, and a kitchen. The kitchen was real little.

Mama hated to leave friends and kinfolk, but I think she looked forward to moving to town. Her life was a little easier work wise. We had running water in the kitchen, but we didn't have an inside toilet and she still had to wash clothes in a wash pot.

There was a stable behind the house big enough for Daddy's horses and a cow. For a while Daddy plowed gardens for people; he did pretty good like that, but he had a hard time finding enough hay and feed for the animals. Sometimes he would see where somebody had mowed their yard and he'd get that to feed them.

Later on he worked at other jobs, but Daddy never worked in the cotton mill.


I was excited about going to a new school. I knew it would be different—a lot bigger. Robbins Elementary School wasn't more than six or seven blocks from our house; so I went to Robbins, what rest of school I went.

At Lick Creek when you got through with a book and went on to another one you was in another grade. At Robbins everybody in your room was in the same grade and on the same place in the same subject. They told me I was in the sixth grade at Lick Creek. At Robbins School I ended up in the fifth grade. Well, it was better, 'cause I didn't know some of the things they were learning. I managed. It was a little bit hard on me, but I loved it.

We lived on Salisbury Road for a year or so and then we moved about four blocks to the other side of South Main Street in a house on West 11$^{th}$ Avenue. It was a large house painted white with a little barn out back. It was the first painted house we ever lived in.

Daddy raised a garden. He always raised a garden. Most everybody made space enough to raise a garden. Even after Daddy had to get rid of the horses, he got a little push plow and he would till up a little track, just a little at a time, or else he would dig it up with a shovel so he could raise a garden. Sometimes he would get a pig and fatten it up with table scraps. There was always somebody to kill it for you. We were half country and half town.

The house was big enough that Julie and Lela came back home to live so they could save money on board. Virgie didn't come back home. She went to live with a family of Bean's that had originally come from Denton near Healing Springs. They had a daughter named Elva that was about the same age as Virgie. Elva and Virgie had become good friends, so Elva's mama asked Virgie to come live with them so Elva would have someone her age to be around.

Later on, the Bean's moved to High Point and Virgie went along with them. She got a job in the Staley's Silk Mill and lived over there up until after she and Elva both married. They remained friends and kept in touch even after that.

Lela was the first one of us to get married. She married Will Koonts. He came a-dating Lela after she moved back home. Will had a brother named Lon—just L-o-n. Lon had epilepsy.

Julie married next, to Gray Lanning. She met him at work. Lela and Julie both married mill boys. They both got married in town at the justice of the peace. Poor people didn't have big weddings. I liked both their husbands.

While Virgie was living in High Point with the Beans she met a boy named Raymond Templeton at a church meeting. Raymond grew up on his daddy's farm between Mocksville and Statesville and had left the farm to go to High Point an work in Staley's Silk Mill. When Virgie first met Raymond neither one knew at the time that the other worked at the silk mill. Raymond worked nights, Virgie worked days. They started dating, and then married. They had one son, William; they call him Bill.

*P*

As a girl, I loved to go to the theater. Saturday was school day at the theater for children twelve years old or younger and school children got a special prize. I'd go every chance I got. Mary Pickford was one of my favorite movie stars.

The first time I was invited to go to the show with a boy I was about twelve.

Mama said, "Well if Fred can go along, you can go."

So Fred went with us.

The first wedding I ever saw was at the show. A group of actors come to town with a Vaudeville show. Two of the actors in the show got married on stage after the play. It wasn't fancy like you see now, but it was the first wedding I ever saw.

Every fall, we'd have the county fair. They'd come to town with tents and rides and have a Ferris wheel and Merry-Go-Round, or Carousel. They'd have little rides for the little children to ride on too. Mama wouldn't let us go off to the fair by ourselves, so I'd go with some of the family.

I couldn't ride most of the rides because they made me sick. But I liked to ride the Ferris wheel. I could ride that and that didn't bother me, but when I rode the Carousel, I'd get sick. I can't even rock in a rocking chair now because it makes me dizzy.

They had eating booths all around and tents with games—games where you knock stuff down and get prizes, dishes and things. Cupie dolls were a big thing then. They were about nine or ten inches tall and made of, I don't know exactly what, but it was something breakable, maybe a ceramic.

The Cupie dolls were prizes for either throwing baseballs or shooting at one of the galleries. Julie's husband, Gray, won two Cupie dolls in one night. I was with them that night. He gave Julie one and me one. Julie kept her doll. She kept it in the box and kept it up on a shelf and wouldn't let the children touch it. I kept mine until after I was married. As the children came along the doll didn't last long. I never had a place to put it up where the children couldn't get to it.

I don't know what ever happened to Julie's doll. I guess one of her children has it.

There were a whole lot of little sideshows. They would have

something spectacular to draw the people in, like a two-headed calf, or people they claimed were Siamese twins, but you could tell they weren't together. I mean their bodies wasn't together.

They had the shows with dancing and then they had some you could go back in there and see things. I never went back in there. I don't really know what they were about, whether it was odd people or what it was, but they would have the signs outside to attract the people to come in.

They had a motorcycle race inside this thing—this round cage like thing. We sat up on bleachers to see it. They'd start out at the bottom with their motorcycle and just keep on going around that cage 'til it looked like they were going to come out the top. It would just scare you to death.

Alma at age fourteen

One year they had a horse that jumped off a high platform into a tank of water. The ramp was maybe fifteen or more foot high. I don't remember if they had a man leading the horse up or not, but the horse would just run up the ramp and jump off into a large tank of water. That was in the mid-twenties when I was a child of about fourteen that I saw that.

At fourteen I started baby-sitting for Lee and Nannie. Mama needed the money. I went back and forth from home to Lee's house. I didn't get to go to school much after that. So since I was missing so much school, I lost interest and quit. I had finished the sixth grade and went a little bit of the seventh. Mama should have whipped me for not going to school, but she was glad for me to quit and go to work because she needed the money. My education would have done me a lot more good, but I didn't realize it and Mama didn't have the interest. Frances quit a couple years after I did. Fred went through high school. He graduated. Cora and Flora graduated too.

Cora and Flora

Cora and Flora were real close when they were growing up. They always stayed together. Mama always dressed them alike. The city schools were the only schools Cora and Flora ever went to. The teachers at Robbins School called them the Gold Dust

Twins. Gold Dust was the name of a popular washing powders back then. The box had a picture of some little twin girls on it dressed alike called the Gold Dust Twins.

At Robbins, one Halloween, the teacher had Cora and Flora to dress up alike and had them to stand up and said, "See! Here is the Gold Dust twins!"

Back then some of the washing powders had a free gift inside—small pieces of chinaware like a free cup or dish, cereal bowl or something like that. No big pieces. If you got the big pieces you had to save coupons to get them as premiums.

Mama bought coffee that had coupons on it. She saved them and sent off and got a gold locket about the size of a quarter. She gave it to me. She put it on a ribbon and I wore it around my neck. I still have it somewhere, but the lid won't stay shut now. It has a little diamond in it—just a little speck of one. It was from *Arbuckle's Coffee*. This was way back in the late teens. We still lived across Cabin Creek at that time. I don't know why she gave it to me.

Cora and Flora didn't graduate from school the same year because they separated them and put Cora in a higher grade. Flora couldn't learn quite as fast as Cora could. When Cora graduated she got a scholarship to go to Brevard College in Black Mountain, North Carolina. She took business courses. When she graduated she got a good job working in an office.

# 13

In the mid 1920s land was bought, about five miles out of town on the corner of Highway 8 and Linwood Road, from a Taylor man to build a Junior Order Children's Home to house and care for orphaned children. People in Lexington donated money to buy the land. The Junior Order Children's Home was a nation-wide organization and Lexington being selected for a home was an honor.

The Taylor land had originally belonged to Odell's ancestors. It was initially part of the Peter Owen plantation, Odell's great-grandfather. Peter's son Alfred, Odell's grandfather, and Alfred's brother, David, got that part of the plantation when Peter died. David sold his land to somebody and Taylor's got a-hold of it.

The whole town took interest in the children's home. People would ride down there during the week to watch them build on it, and on Sundays to see the progress. Young people from town would walk down there to look it over and so on. Me and some of my friends would go down there. Sometimes we'd get a ride with somebody. Sometimes we'd get out and walk down there.

Walking for miles was nothing to us. As a teenager a bunch of us girls would just get out on Sunday's and just walk. That's all we had to do. It was me and Frances and just whoever would come around.

We had friends in Thomasville, about ten miles away, and lots of Sundays we'd walk over

Frances and Alma as teenagers

there to visit. If we didn't get a ride back home, we would walk back. Walking ten miles—that wasn't nothing. We walked all afternoon. We kept out of Mama's hair like that. We didn't want to stay home anyway.

After they finished building the Junior Order Children's Home they brought children in from all over. They bused children down here from a home in Ohio.

They bought that land and built that home for the children. Lots of people still live in Lexington that grew up there.

Before we moved to Lexington, I don't know exactly when, Mama and Daddy both got saved. In town, they both started going to the First Baptist Church.

As far as I can remember they weren't the *go get 'em* Christians and all, but just the regular every day steady. Daddy took his church going more serious than Mama did. He went to church every Sunday, but sometimes Mama didn't feel like going so she didn't go. But Daddy *always* went.

I went to First Baptist, too. That's where I was baptized and first joined the church. I joined when I was about thirteen or fourteen years old. But I guess I was about eleven or twelve when I first realized I was a Christian. It was at a revival meeting at Baker's Springs Church. That's the first time I realized and accepted Christ.

After I got a little older, I quit going to First Baptist and started going to the Trinity Methodist Church on South Main Street. It's a brick church now, but it was a frame church at that time. I went there until I got married.

The best advice I ever got from my mama and Daddy was to go to church.

When I was sixteen, we moved up on South Main Street in a house where the Budweiser Beer warehouse is now. We were living there when I got married.

It was a nice large white frame house that set up on a big high bank with steps that went up from the street to get to it. Different ones talk about when South Main Street wasn't paved, but it was paved when we lived there. That was around 1925 or 26.

To start with we still had the outside toilet, but they finally took a little pantry out on the porch and fixed a toilet in it. In the wintertime it would freeze up. Boy, was it cold!

There was a baseball field near our back yard. Wenonah Cotton Mill built it up and sponsored a team. The ball field was just an open field with a couple of benches to sit on if you wanted to. They didn't charge to watch the games or anything.

The team was mostly mill workers. They worked ten hours a day and played ball after they got

Alma

off work in their spare time. Lela's husband, Will, played on the team. They played other teams from all over. They were good.

Somewhere along about that time Mama's sister, Aunt Freda, moved to High Point. Her husband, Will, got a job over there, so they rented a house and moved over there. Mama let me go along with them. I stayed six months, I guess, over there.

On Saturdays, Aunt Freda and me would ride to town on the trolley to look around just for the fun of it. One Saturday I got me a bag of chocolate candy. I liked chocolate candy and I filled up on it on the way home. It made me sick. Boy, was I sick. I didn't want any more chocolate candy for a long time.

Aunt Freda let me get a job in a hosiery mill learning how to run a looper; that's what sews up the toes in socks or hose. They would teach you how to run the looper for free. You didn't get paid anything, but as you begin to learn, they would pay you a little bit, but not much. I worked on regular cotton hose and what was supposed to be silk or somethin' nother. I learned both of them.

They were expecting me to stay on and work with them after I learned, but I didn't. When I got finished learning, I quit and come back home to Lexington. That's the first I ever worked at public work.

Alma

After I came home, I got a job running a looper at Shoaf's Hosiery Mill. It wasn't hard work, but it was tedious. I had to put the toe of the hose on these fine needles. The toe had something like a band that goes along the top. If I held it up I could see a little line. I had to put the toe of the hose on the needles along that line and I had to hit the little holes just right or there would be a hole in the hose. Usually if I hit one right, the rest would just go

100

on. The cotton ones was okay, but the silk ones were harder to work with. They were a pain.

I didn't work there long before I left the hosiery mill and got a job at the Wabena Yarn Mill on West 11th Avenue. Daddy worked some for the Wabena mill, too. He served as a security guard. I worked six days a week, ten hours a day for fifteen dollars. I got half of what I made and gave Daddy the rest.

The Wabena Mill made yarn for the carpet trade. They'd spin cotton into thread. My job was running the thread onto spools or cones. I had to keep the spools threaded so they would fill up and change them when they run full. It wasn't hard, but sometimes it'd keep you running. Sometimes the spools would fill up

Alma

in, it seemed like, minutes. I'd take the full ones off and put the empty ones on and thread them so they would fill up again. Some days we were run so hard keeping them changed out that we might not even get any lunch. We'd have to shut down if we did.

When I got paid, I would go to the store and buy me clothes—dresses. Most of the time I got my dresses in town at Efrid's Department store. They carried a pretty good line. My

—sister, Lela, could sew good and sometimes I would buy cloth and she would make dresses for me.

I worked at the Wabena on up until after I married Odell. During the depression the Wabena closed. I guess they couldn't sell enough yarn to keep it going. Somebody bought it and turned it into a place that made little cedar chests. When that give out, Franklin Shockey bought it and started making furniture.

After I married, Mama and Daddy moved several more times. They moved down on Robbins Street, then back up on South Main Street into a big house right across from the ballpark. It was a frame house, a fairly nice house. From there, Mama and Daddy moved up on East 4$^{th}$ Avenue near the Piedmont Funeral Home. They were living there on East 4$^{th}$ Avenue when I had my third baby.

From there they moved to High Point. In High Point, Daddy worked at Merita Paint as a sweeper man. In all his jobs Daddy never run a machine of any kind.

# 14

The first time I saw Odell was in 1926 at a medicine show. They used to have the old traveling medicine shows that would come to town and have music and sing and all, sort of like the vaudeville shows. One came to town and set up there where Model Cleaners and all was built—at the corner of South Main Street and Cotton Grove Road. That was an open field then.

Everybody would see them when they moved in. They would be painted up like colored people and get up on their truck or platform, and start playing their music and go to singing and dancing and selling their medicine. And of course everybody would just go ganging up to them to see what was going on, particularly the young ones, but a whole lot of the older ones came. A whole lot of the older ones, they'd buy the liniment. I don't know whether it ever did them any good or not.

I don't remember whether it was spring or fall, but it was

warm weather and a bunch of us girls, we were wanting to go somewhere to have something new to do. So, when something like the medicine show came to town, we went out there to see what it was all about.

It was me, my sister Frances, Essie Hedrick, and I can't remember exactly who the other one was at the time. We were all about sixteen, something like that.

Essie and me were close friends during our school days and part of our teenage years—up until she got married. She married a Leonard.

Well, there were these boys there, and they were in their late teens and they came around where we was. It was Odell and his friend Wilber, and I forget who the others were. Essie knew them—knew Odell and these boys, had known them all her life— at least part of them. Anyway, we and they got to talking, and we all got to talking and they took us for a ride. Odell had a car. I don't know what kind of car Odell was driving then, but anyway we all got to talking and he took us for a ride. There was enough for all of us to have a partner right then. But I didn't partner with Odell.

At the medicine show was the first time I had seen Odell. I didn't even know who he was 'til we went out there. He was a nice looking boy, tall with brown hair, and a nice smile, but he didn't strike me at first as a boy I wanted to know. He was just another boy—just one of the group of boys.

I remember the boy that partnered with me that first night; years later he said, "Odell stole my girl! You was my girl!"

I didn't care anything about him. I dated other boys, but they were too smoochie. I couldn't stand that. Maybe I was too tidy. I don't know. Some of them know how to kiss right, but some of them—it was just like eating a sandwich. That didn't appeal to me at all.

Odell was nice. He wasn't loud or talkative very much. Wasn't pushy. That suited me. The first time Odell asked me for a date it was just, "Come on lets go for a ride." Or something like that, and that was all.

So, from that first meeting we started dating. It was off and on, nothing regular. It didn't start all at once.

Odell was living with his parents on their farm and working for RB Miller Wholesale delivering vegetables and fruit to stores.

The main office for the wholesale was in Salisbury. The Lexington branch, where Odell worked, was in a warehouse off West 5$^{th}$ Avenue across from the Southbound Railroad depot. It had a large basement in it where they kept the bananas and other perishable fruit so they would last longer.

Odell would go out for RB and get the orders from the stores—what they would want. Then the next day he would take the orders back to them in the truck. So, he was both the salesman and the deliverer.

RB had some cows in a field right beside the Wabena mill. He made hay on a tract of land right there too. Sometimes he would send Odell and some of his boys to look after the cows, put them in the barn and things like that, sometimes he'd send them down there to make the hay. If we had a minute to spare, some of us girls would look out the window of the mill and see them working. We'd get there in the window and watch them and all. We'd laugh and make out like we was waving to them. Odell and me had dated a few times.

Odell was always a hard worker. As a boy he raised turkeys to sell. He'd let them just rambled loose over the whole farm. The foxes got some of them. Odell hunted the foxes, and what turkeys he could save from the foxes he sold.

One time he sold a turkey that weighed thirty some pounds. The man that bought it said that was the toughest turkey he'd ever got a-hold of. He sold some to the grocery stores up town—like *Conrad and Hinkle*, and *Picketts*.

Odell's daddy, JD, had a team of horses and a scoop to scoop up dirt. As a boy, Odell helped his daddy do work for the road people—hauling dirt to put on the streets in Lexington before they had cement.

I can remember as a child back when the streets were dirt and people use to ride horse-drawn buggies to town. In wet times the roads would get ruts and they'd have to put down planks or somethin' nother in the streets for people to walk on to get them up out of the mud.

The courthouse and the old upper part of town was built up before my time, but the lower end of town down around the Carolina Theater was built up since I can remember.

106

Odell's daddy had a threshing machine and threshed people's wheat during the summer. Odell used to tell about going off on wheat threshing trips with his daddy and his brothers, Will and George, and be gone a week or more at a time.

When he got up older, Odell worked at a furniture factory—I think he said two weeks. He didn't like that, not a little bit, so he quit.

Then he got his chance to work for RB Miller. Joe Taylor, one of his good friends, worked there. Joe told Odell RB was looking for another hand. Odell talked to RB and got the job. In the meantime, Joe wouldn't come in to work sometimes when he was suppose to so RB fired him. That's how Odell's brother, Will, got his job with RB. So, Odell and Will got the jobs. Miller's daughter, Hattie, was the bookkeeper.

Odell was working for RB when he bought his first car. That was around 1925. Arnold Walser was selling cars at his grocery store on the corner of South Main Street and West 11<sup>th</sup> Ave. So Odell went down there and talked to him about buying one on credit.

Walser let him have one for four hundred dollars, a black Ford Roadster. All the cars were black back then. He paid that off in a little over a year, 'cause he was working and living at home and didn't have a lot of expenses.

Odell was real particular with that car. He rubbed on it and wouldn't let any dust get on it. It had a cloth top with black curtains at the windows that you could put down to keep the rain and cold out—like a buggy. They just snapped on sort of like snapping up a tent.

At that time, not many of the boys had cars. They couldn't afford them. Later on, people would buy the cars and didn't know how to run them or take care of them and they would sell them for just about nothing.

Odell and Alma on top of Pilot Mountain

On dates, sometimes we'd go to the Carolina picture show, but Odell didn't like the show. Sometimes we'd just ride around. Sometimes there would be a baseball game, or sometimes we'd meet at people's houses.

Odell's brother, Will, started dating my sister Frances. We double dated quite a bit. Will didn't have a car and double dating made it convenient for him. Sometimes we'd even carry another couple along in that little ole two-seater roadster. How we packed in there, I don't know. They'd throw us under the jailhouse now. That little ole seat was tight for two and we'd put three in one seat and two on top. We'd pile in and even go to the mountains sometimes.

Six of us went from Lexington to Salisbury one Halloween

just to see what we could see. It was me and Odell, Will and Frances, Essie Hedrick and I don't know who she was dating at the time. Boy, we packed in there. We were all the time doing somethin' nother.

We dated with another couple where the boy's name was Odell too. But we never did date or pair up with Jesse or Joe Taylor; that was Odell's life long friends. We never did date with them. I don't know why.


Odell and me would date and then we'd stop, we'd date and then we'd stop. Went on that way for three years I reckon. It finally ended up us running off to York, South Carolina to get married. We didn't tell nobody.

Odell wore a suit. I wore a blue dress that I bought at the store. My hair was shoulder length. I fixed it combed to the side and let it lay in natural waves around my face.

Later on, I loaned my dress to Odell's sister Clara to wear for somethin' nother and before she brought it back the house caught fire and burned and burned my dress.

There was no ring, no honeymoon. Odell didn't want it no how. Odell didn't believe in things like that. Anything he had to spend for, he didn't want.

I got a wedding ring, but Odell didn't buy it for me. I went to the jewelry store and bought it myself the Christmas after we got married.

First, I bought Odell a nice billfold and he refused it. He didn't like it. It was a real nice billfold, but he didn't like it. So I took it back, took the money and went to Parkers Jewelry and bought me a wedding ring. I didn't wear it much 'cause it would wear on my finger. I still have it in there somewhere.

We spent our wedding night in Asheville in a hotel. I had never spent the night in a hotel before. We came back to Lexington the next day to live with Odell's parents. A whole lot of girls went to live with their husband's family back then. They didn't have enough to go out on their own with, no furniture, no nothing.

We got married Wednesday, June 28th, 1929, my nineteenth birthday. Odell turned twenty-four three months later in September. We were five years apart.

# 15

The Owen farmhouse set way back off the road with a long curving driveway that led up to it. It was an ordinary white T-shaped two-story farmhouse with a porch across the front of it. An unpainted rough wide-board shed, big enough to park two cars in, set out in the front yard at the driveway. There were two big maples and a mimosa tree between the house and the driveway. The backyard had another big maple tree, a pear tree, several out buildings, a barn, a combination grainy-corncrib and a smoke house.

The front door of the house opened into a hallway with bedrooms off to each side. Beyond that was the dining room. It had a porch to its left, then beyond that was the kitchen with a porch off to the right. The dining room also served as the family gathering room.

When Odell was a teenager, him and his brother Will, built

two rooms in the attic. The house wasn't built for upstairs rooms. You could stand upright in the middle of them, but if you got over on the sides you couldn't. It didn't make very good living up there. The steps to go upstairs were in the front hall. Boy, were they steep! Somehow, they misjudged the planning of them and they were very steep to go up and down.

The bedroom on the left as you go in the front door was mine and Odell's room. It was a large room with a fireplace and big windows on both outside walls. One window looked out onto the front porch and the other to the side yard. We didn't buy any furniture. We used theirs.

I didn't know Odell's parents very well before we were married. I hadn't been down there but a few times. They went to Center Hill Baptist Church and while we were dating, Center Hill was having prayer meetings in the homes. Odell's mama, she would volunteer for them to come to her house. Odell's mama was a Christian; JD claimed to be, but he couldn't leave the bottle alone.

One night while we were dating Odell took me to his house to a prayer meeting. That was the first time I met Odell's parents. I don't know why he took me; we didn't stay long. That was a long time before we got married.

Odell had two brothers, George and Will and three sisters, Leora, Bessy and Clara. Leora and Bessy were married. Leora married Henry Warfford. Bessy's husband was Carl Wrenn. George, Will and Clara were the only ones still living at home.

Clara wasn't at home very long though. The following year she married Charlie Davis.

I had a good relationship with Odell's sisters. They were all nice to me. There wasn't any problems. If there was any problem, I guess it was me, because I was inexperienced.

I liked Martha, Odell's mother. She was nice. She was talkative. She liked people and she was always friendly with them. In a way she was a little bit out going, but not too much. Odell nicknamed me Sally, he called me that before and after we were married. Martha called me Sally some too. Everybody else called me Alma, but nobody had the whole name. They would leave the L out and say, *am-mer.*

Martha was a stout broad shouldered woman, a hard worker. I'd say she'd weigh close to two hundred pounds, but she was tall, taller than JD, tall enough that she didn't look fat. Her hair was a light brown. 'Course it might have been darker when she was young. It had some natural wave to it, I'd say some life in it, but it wasn't curly. She wore it long and balled up on the back of her head. She wore her skirts and dresses about mid-calf. That was the style for women.

JD was short and thin, maybe five foot seven or eight, he wasn't as tall as Odell. Will looked more like JD than Odell did.

Most of the time JD was dressed in pants and a shirt. He did some trading of horses and things like that. For work in the field he wore overalls and a hat.

JD called Martha by her name, but some called her Mat. Odell's Uncle George's wife was named Martha too, so some

113

called Odell's mama Mat to keep them separated. Martha called Odell's daddy JD or John.

Martha was five years older than JD. She was fifty-seven when Odell and me got married. JD was fifty-two.

JD drank and had a temper, but a lot of it, I think, was just a whole lot of show. I wasn't afraid of him. He was all right in his way. He had come up rough.

JD's daddy, Alfred, was born in 1817, and raised south of Lexington in Linwood on his daddy Peter Owen's large plantation. Alfred had brothers. I remember hearing of David, but I don't know the rest or exactly how many brothers and sisters he had.

Alfred Owen

Alfred served in the Civil War. He was in his late forties when he volunteered to fight. Records show that he served in the Cavalry. I've got an old two by three inch daguerreotype picture of Alfred in his Confederate uniform. The picture has dimmed over the years, but you can see him. He's sitting sideways in a chair with one arm resting up on the back and wearing a rumpled Confederate uniform and hat. He's slim, scruffy looking, with a stubble of a beard. His eyes are strong, piercing, almost evil eyes. Odell looks a lot like Alfred.

Odell had reproductions made of Alfred's picture and gave them out to all the children. Glenn's wife, Nancy, went by it to paint a large two and a-half by three foot portrait of him. Odell asked Nancy for it and hung it out in our hall. When the grandchildren came to visit, they wouldn't play out there near where it was because of how Alfred's eyes starred down so mean. I give it back to Nancy when Odell died.

Odell used to tell a story about Alfred that was told around in his family, about how one day before he went off to the Civil War, he saw a child, a girl, named Amanda Rowe—they told that she was just a toddler at the time—and Alfred says, "I'm going to marry that girl." And he did!

Old marriage records show that after the war, in August of 1876, Amanda and Alfred were married. Amanda was twenty-one years old and Alfred was fifty-eight, thirty-seven years apart in age.

Alfred lived eleven years after the marriage. They had four children together, William, John David (JD), George and Peter.

When Alfred died, Amanda buried him on the plantation in the Owen family graveyard and marked his grave with a Confederate tombstone. The inscription reads: "In memory of Alfred Owen, Co. F., N.C. Cav. C.S.A."

The graveyard, which is about half an acre in size, holds over a hundred Owen family graves dating from the early to the late 1800s, and also some slave graves.

As years passed and family members died, the Owen estate was divided many times. By the early 1900s the tract of land with the graveyard on it had been sold to someone outside the family. So the graveyard was abandoned as a family burial place and left unattended.

Odell knew about the graveyard from his daddy and told the children about it. In the 1960s, some of them were old enough to be curious about it and went down there and hunted around until they found it.

It was hard to recognize it as a graveyard because of all the big trees and vines that had took it over. Some of the graves had been vandalized. Alfred's grave was dug into, his tombstone was broken and part of his marker was missing. Most of the other tombstones were either broken, sunk into the ground or just laying about in the weeds with no one knowing where they belonged. A good number of the graves were noticed only by a depression in the ground.

Amanda remarried to a Styers man—Sam Styers. She had three daughters by him, twins Mary and Maude, and then Adie.

Styers made it hard on Alfred's boys. He didn't want all those children to raise. He finally boarded Alfred's boys out to different families that took them in and worked them. JD was boarded out to work for a Burkhart family. All of them stayed at different places—one at one place and one at another. This caused a lot of resentment between Styers and the boys. They didn't get to see their mama or each other very much growing up.

William died while he was young. He was riding a horse on the plantation somewhere and fell off and broke a bone, maybe in his leg, but I don't know for sure. It didn't kill him right then; he lived a while, but he never did walk anymore. Back then doctors did what they could, but they didn't have the means to do much.

Before William died, JD bought a rocking chair for him to sit in. After William died JD got the chair back. When JD died his daughter Leora got the chair. I don't know where it is now. I guess one of the children has it.

When JD married Martha, they moved in a house beside his mama and "Old Man Styers," as they called him, on the Alfred Owen home place. Odell was born while they were living there.

Martha told it that when Odell was a baby he had long hair that lay in big pretty curls—just like a girls.

She said, "one day I left Odell with his Grandma Styers to go to Lexington for somethin' nother, so when I came back Amanda had cut Odell's long hair off."

She said she just cried. She took up some of his curls and saved a little piece of them. I still have it in there somewhere, but I don't remember where it's at. It's

JD and his mother, Amanda Owen Styers

just a little twist of hair about as big as your little finger tied with a little string.

117

I've got a baby dress that Odell wore too. Back then boys wore long dresses. They didn't wear them all the time; they must have been just for show. It's white with lace at the top and ruffles around the bottom. They wore the dresses 'til they were two year old or more—walking around in a long dress. They made kids miserable. It's been a long time since I looked at it. I didn't get it until later on, so none of my children wore it. I wouldn't have put it on them anyway. It was much to long for them to crawl in.

When Amanda died JD and his brothers got the land. Alfred had willed it that way, to be divided between the children. JD got a tract of wooded acreage, Peter got the home place and George got the rest.

JD sold his part. He was having so much trouble living beside old man Styers 'til he sold his part to his brother Peter and bought a farm on New Jersey Church Road. That's where Odell and his brothers and sisters were raised and where Odell was living when we got married.

Years later, PPG bought the Alfred Owen home place from the Peter Owen family to build their large plant down there on New Jersey Church Road. Uncle George didn't sell his to PPG though. He did finally sell it to a Smith man.

# 16

I first knew I was pregnant when my periods stopped. I was nervous, because I was going into something I didn't know nothing about. I never was taught about being pregnant. My mama didn't tell me nothing about it. Mama was bashful about things like that. She didn't want to talk about it. She didn't tell me nothing about it—nobody didn't tell me nothing about it.

I told Odell my periods had stopped, so I guess I was pregnant. He wasn't too happy. He wasn't ready for a family yet. When Mama found out I was pregnant, she was mad at me. Some of my sisters were happy and some were not. Odell's mama didn't have anything to say one-way or the other. It was a lonely time.

I went to the doctor up town, Dr. Sowers. First time I went I was scared. I didn't know nothing about going to the doctor. I didn't go to the doctor very much the whole time I was pregnant, just when Odell wanted to take me. But I got along all right.

Didn't have any problems.

For maternity clothes, I just wore something that hung loose, that was the way pregnant women dressed then, they didn't want nobody to see their shape.

While I was pregnant, Dr. Sowers got killed in a car accident. He was going out on a call and somebody run into him, or he run into somebody, I don't know which. Anyway he got killed. He was down on Salisbury Road at the Grubb place. After he died his nephew, Dr. Ed Cathell, took his place and delivered the baby. I had the baby at home.

When you have a baby at home, about a month or so in advance, you have to prepare for it. I read a book to know how to do. It said to prepare a pad to lay on to protect the bed during delivery. It told me what I needed and so on, but half of it I didn't need.

What I did was, I just doubled up an old sheet and tacked it together so it would make a little pad to go under me to keep the bed from getting messed up. It had to be thrown out anyway. Right after the baby comes the bed has to be cleaned up so you can lay in it. Other than that, that's the only thing I had to get ready—except for the baby some clothes. I had to be sure the baby had clothes to put on after it was born and cleaned up. If you went to the hospital you didn't have to fix the bed and all that, but I never went to the hospital for any of my babies. Odell said it cost too much.

Lela and Will were living with Mama when Lela's first baby,

Lois, was born. Lois was Mama's first grandchild. I was still living at home then. I might have been fifteen years old, something like that.

Old Dr. Vestal was Lela's doctor.

When it got time for the baby to be born, the doctor, he come around and told Mama, says, "I got to have some hot water."

So, he asked for hot water, so she went in the kitchen and come back with boiling hot water.

He stuck his hands in there and said, "Damn! I didn't mean for you to scald me!"

That got a-way with Mama so bad. She didn't know what to think. She was halfway all excited anyway.

He said hot water, so she gave him hot water.

Mama said, "He didn't need to talk so hateful."

Julie's oldest son, Ralph, and Lois were born at Mama's house. Lois is a year or so older than Ralph. I tended to them when they would let me.


I remember going into labor. I went into labor late in the evening. My water broke before the doctor ever got there.

When the doctor comes out to deliver the baby he usually brings someone to help him. The help was just who ever would come to help. Sometimes his sister would come, but sometimes a friend would come. Odell's mama was there, but she didn't help. She wasn't in the room. Odell was around. He would come in and then leave. He couldn't stand being in there with me. It was lonely with only strangers.

It was nearly all night 'til the baby was born. I had a hard time because the baby was so large, but it was born healthy. It was a boy. He was born March 31, 1930 and weighed eleven pounds. 'Course they weighed him on hand scales, that might a-been correct and it might a-not. After he was born, they bathed him with a washcloth in warm water and baby oil. That's the way it was done. The baby oil helped get the mess off.

It's not hard to do. I was over at Odell's sister Clara's when one of her children was born. I had never even seen a baby like that before and they handed it to me to clean up. I had the warm water and the little cloth so I just bathed it best I knowed how. I guess it was all right. The doctor didn't say nothing.

After my baby was born, the doctor told me to lay in bed nine days, but I didn't. I got up and did what I wanted to do. I tried breast-feeding him, but my milk didn't agree so I had to put him on cow milk. I never breast-fed any of my children.

Odell wouldn't help me name him. Odell's mama named him. She said, "Name him Foy!"

Foy

So, I just added the Henderson. Henderson was Odell's Grandpa Snider's name. Martha was a Snider. Odell's Grandpa Snider's full name was David Henderson Snider, but they called him Hense. He lived from March 11, 1835 to November 18, 1912. Odell's Grandma Snider's name was Caroline Lomax Snider. She lived from April 22, 1830 to August 18, 1914. So, I didn't know them.

Martha had a couple brothers and three sisters. I met one of them, but the others I didn't know. Her family was from Churchland, about twelve miles west of Lexington. They're all buried out there in a big cemetery on Highway 150. Two churches are across the road from the cemetery. One's a primitive Baptist and I don't know what the other one is.

Odell's mama gave me a quilt that Odell's Grandma Snider made. It's in the chest trunk. It's a bright yellow and green. It's over a hundred and thirty years old.

Before Foy was born I made gowns and diapers for him. I didn't buy anything. The depression was coming along and cloth was getting cheap, so I bought the material and made them. Martha had a pedal sewing machine, and Mama had taught me how to sew a little bit, but mostly I just picked it up on my own. I would read everything I could about it.

For diapers, I took cloth and cut it into squares, and hemmed it. For baby blankets, I cut a piece of flannel into sizes I wanted and hemmed around it.

When Foy was a couple months old, I made him a little romper suit. I made it out of a print material that had little toys and things on it. I put it on him and took him up to Mamas'. Grandpa's brother, my great uncle, was up there and he didn't like the looks of the romper suit.

He says, "What are you trying to do make a man out of him before he gets a chance to grow." Says, "Babies ain't supposed to wear that kind of clothes."

They were putting prints on children at that time, but he was just blunt about it.

Alma

I continued to work at the Wabena Yarn Mill up as long as I could before Foy was born. After he was born I tried it again. Mama kept him while I worked. I had to get Foy up out of bed, take him up to Mama's, then go on to work and come back to Mamas' after work and get him. Odell, if he didn't forget me, would take me back and forth.

Mama kept Foy for one week. He got a cold and Odell said, "No more." Said, "If you're going to work You'll have to go to town and stay."

I might a-done better if I had. So, that was the end of my working.

# 17

When Foy was about a year old, we moved out from Odell's parents into the Sides house, that big two-story frame house right in front of the Junior Order Children's Home on Cotton Grove Road. We rented it from Mable Hulin.

C.E. Sides built the house and run a store beside it. At the time he built it, his wife, Lena, was living and their daughters Mable and Gladys were at home. Gladys died when she was just a little girl school age. Mable grew up, went off to college and met and married a Hulin. When her mama and daddy died, the house went to her.

It was painted white with a porch all the way across the front and part way around the back. It was an expensive house when it was built. It was pretty. It had painted floors. They were beautiful. I had never been around anything like that.

Inside the front door was a big hallway with a staircase. The

125

living room was on one side of the hallway and the dining room and kitchen on the other. Upstairs were two bedrooms and a hallway with a banister around the stairwell. It was pretty.

Out behind the house there was a well where we got our water, and an outside toilet. The toilet was just a small shed-like building built over a hole dug in the ground. Inside was a wooden seat built up with a hole cut out in it for you to sit on. For toilet paper, we used the Sears Catalog. It was free.

An outside toilet?—that's a nasty, dirty thing. The smell, the flies and the bugs. It was a good thing when they had to quit using them. On top of being nasty, you had to worry about snakes. One might get there first.

The house had electricity. Sides store, that was right next to us, had electricity run to it, so Sides run it to the house too. I never had electricity before. It wasn't until about 1939 or 40, that electricity came through to most all the rural houses.


Odell bought us some furniture. He bought a bedroom suit, a living room suit, a kitchen cabinet, a three-burner oil stove, a dinning room suit with a small china cabinet and a table and four chairs.

The bedroom suit was a blonde color. It had little circles in the top of the headboard like lace; then the footboard, it bowed a little bit. It had a dresser with drawers, a vanity and a wardrobe to hang our clothes in. The vanity had three folding mirrors with a stand on each side joined by a low shelf in the middle. The mirrors came down to the stands. It was second hand, but it was pretty.

The living room suit was a brown print color. It was just one chair and the settee. I don't know if the living room suit was second hand or not, but it was cheap. You can tell the cheap ones, made cheap; they don't last.

We lived in three rooms, the kitchen and dining room and a bedroom. It was just easier to heat and keep up three rooms than to try to keep up the whole house. We used the dining room for our living room.

I didn't know how to keep house, take care of floors and things like that, and I messed it up. I had never lived in a house that nice. I had never been around painted floors and I didn't know how to take care them.

Mama always cleaned floors with homemade lye soap and water. She would just dump water on the floor and scrub it. She had plain unpainted floors and the lye soap would clean them and make them look pretty.

Most everybody used lye soap for one thing or 'nother to clean around the house. Boy, it would take the dirt out of clothes, but it would eat the clothes too. It would also work on your hands and made them look rough.

So I mopped my floors like always, with lye soap and water. After I cleaned my floors, I learned that when you put a little lye soap in the water and mop the floor it will come clean, but if you had painted floors, you didn't have them then. It took the finish right off.

Mable come in one day and said, "Ruined my floors!

Somebody ruined my floors!"

I didn't tell her I done it. I didn't want her to know I was that dumb. Our floors had always been just wood, no finish.

That same year Frances and Will got married. They rented them a house close to the forks of number 8 Highway and Fairview Drive. They stayed there one night; I'm not sure they stayed one night. Odell accused them of being afraid. They moved out and moved in with us in the extra rooms. They lived with us until after their first child, Roy, was born.

On the 22$^{nd}$ day of June 1932 I had Macks. Foy was two years old. I named him Macks, and Odell's mama added the Howard to it. So, we named him Howard Macks.

Foy age 3

Foy had a little wagon that Odell had bought him, and sometimes I would put a little pillow in it and lay Macks on it and pull him around with me while I cleaned house. One day I was upstairs working and had Macks out in the hall in the wagon where it would be cool. Well, here come Foy and pushed the wagon all the way around the banisters and all the way down the steps. It didn't hurt Macks though. He cried a little bit because it scared him, but he was okay.

By 1932, the depression was coming on strong and RB Miller didn't have enough work for both Odell and Will. RB would let one work for a little while and then the other work a day or so. It kept on that way, so finally he laid Odell off. Somehow a-nother he chose Will over Odell. Will didn't work much longer either. When RB let him go, Will and Frances moved to Virginia. Will got a job up there in a shipping yard, but they didn't stay long. When they came back they moved in with Odell's mama.

Odell got a job working at the Junior Order Children's Home teaching the boys how to farm. He'd take them out to the fields and teach them how to work the crop.

As a boy Odell did farm work for old-man John Lopp Sr.. I guess old-man Lopp was the one that really taught him farming. He taught him more about farming than his daddy did. His son, John Lopp Jr., was Odell's good friend.

Odell didn't work for the Junior Order Home long 'til he decided to go into farming for himself. Will decided he wanted to farm too, so Odell and Will bought a tractor together. During the depression was a good time to buy a tractor. You could get one cheap. Odell started doing custom work for people, plowing or combining, things like that. And that's where he got into farming as his life's work.


Times got so hard that we couldn't pay the rent on the Sides house, so we moved. We moved back down to Odell's daddy's farm into what they called the *little-house*. It was a small three room shack like house down in the bottom of the pasture—'cross the branch down there. It was two rooms with a small kitchen built on the backside.

Odell's daddy had the little-house built after we were married

129

for a family he got to come help him on the farm. He didn't have nowhere for them to live, so he built up this little shed-like house for them. They had moved out of the little-house, so we moved in. It wasn't big and it wasn't much, but we were to ourself.

It wasn't long after we moved 'til Will decided he was tired of farming. Will wasn't cut out to be a farmer. He knew how to tell you what to do, but he didn't know how to do it.

So Will come around to Odell wanting to sell his part of the tractor. Him and Frances were wanting to move out from Odell's mama's and rent them a house and they needed furniture.

Frances liked my dining room suit, and Will wanted to get out of the farming business, and Odell wanted the tractor. So Odell traded my dining room suit and somethin' nother, I done forgot now what else, for Will's part of the tractor. Odell fixed up a little ole table or somethin' nother for us to eat off of and I just had to make do with what furniture was left. If Odell needed farm equipment, then farm equipment was bought and we did without.

# 18

Macks was just a toddler, about fourteen months old, when I was due with my third baby. So I boarded out Foy and Macks to different ones in the family and went to Mama's house in Lexington on East 4$^{th}$ Avenue until the baby was born.

Odell took Macks down to my sister Julie's. She had two boys, Ralph and Bucky. Bucky was about the same age as Macks. While Macks and Bucky were playing around together, Bucky threw something, a rock or somethin' nother, and hit Macks on the head. Odell went and got him and took him to one of his sisters. I don't remember who kept Foy.

I had my baby on August 23, 1933 and we named him Kenneth Lee. Kenneth was an instrument baby. They had to use forceps to pull him out. He had a little scar on his head, but not very bad.

The children were all healthy, nothing serious except when

diphtheria came along. Macks took the diphtheria and Foy, he took it, and I took it. That is the *awfulest* sore throat I have *ever*. You just can't imagine. You just wanted to tear out your throat. It just hurt and burned. You just wanted to scratch it out.

I don't know how we caught it. We hadn't been anywhere whatsoever, hadn't even been out from the house.

The doctor said. "Well it's just in the air I reckon."

Macks was two years old, just a toddler. He was two in June and this was October when we had the diphtheria. Kenneth was about three months old and he didn't take it, but Macks and Foy and me did. Macks was so bad, but the doctor didn't recognize it.

He came and looked at Macks and said, "He just has a sore throat." said, "He'll be better in a day or so." and just gave him somethin' nother for a sore throat.

Next day Macks was worse. He couldn't swallow. When he tried to swallow the milk would come back out of his nose. Macks got so bad 'til his throat, I guess, swelled shut. Odell went right quick up to Sides grocery store to call the doctor, the store stayed open pretty late and everybody would go up there to make telephone calls. Not many people had phones in their homes.

Odell told the doctor to come as quick as he could get there. When the doctor saw Macks, he got scared. And boy, he got busy! He gave Macks two shots of somethin' nother. It was something they gave for diphtheria. Anyway it was doubled for what he gave Foy and me. We didn't know whether Macks was going to pull through or not. But after that he got all right.

Fourteen months after Kenneth, on October 11, 1934, Thomas was born. I named him Thomas.

Martha said, "Well name him Claude!"

It was somebody she knew sometime a-nother. So, we named him Thomas Claude and called him Tommy.

Seventeen months later, Hazel came along, I had a hard time with Hazel. Hazel was born on the first day of March 1936. Snow was on the ground. Odell went to get a neighbor to come over and then went for the doctor.

The doctor come, but I was having a little problem giving birth to her. He gave me a shot that was supposed to ease my pain, but it didn't, it made it worse. I yelled out and everybody come running to see what was going on.

I didn't want them there and said, "you could a-stayed back a minute!"

She wasn't born right then, but she was born in a little bit. Whatever it was the doctor gave me brought the pains on instead of easing it. I was always kind of curious with that. Sometimes they give something and it will work the other way.

With one of my babies, I don't remember which one, I started having pains late in the evening and thought I was going into labor.

I got everything ready and then I asked them, said, "I want to use the pot."

I sat on the potty, had a bowel movement and then that was it. So, I gave them a false alarm that time.

Odell named Hazel.

He kept on saying, "Name her Hazel."

Every name I'd pick out he'd say, "No, name her Hazel."

That was one of his old school teacher's names. So, we named her Hazel Carolyn. Carolyn was Mama's second name.

I was glad to have a girl, and a little surprised after four boys. I enjoyed fixing Hazel up. I used to make some of the prettiest little dresses for her. I had a little bit of time then, but not much. One dress I made for her, I smocked across the yoke; when Clara saw it, she wanted one for her youngest daughter, Joann. Joann was the same age as Hazel. So, I made her one.

Clara had an older daughter, Doris. Then, every time Clara made something for Doris or Joann, she would come to me saying, "What should I trim this in? What should I trim this in?"

Well, I knew that red went with everything and was easier to say then to try to pick out another color, so I'd say red.

One time she came asking me and said, "And please don't say red."

I didn't realize I could influence her that much. Most people pick out what colors *they* want, not ask somebody else what would you do. So, she never asked me no more.

The little-house had small rooms. With five children we had to stack'em up. We had two or three beds in every room.

The kitchen didn't have running water, so I had to carry water from the spring. The kitchen cook stove furnished heat in the wintertime, but it was so open you could see outdoors through the cracks. You just as well try to heat the outside.

It was hard and we done without. But the older generations done without a whole lot more than I had to. If they could make what they needed, well it was all right, but if they couldn't, well they done without. Sometimes they didn't even have a bed. They'd just threw a straw tick on the floor and slept on that.

To make their straw ticks, they took sheets, sewed them together all the way around and left the top split open. They filled that with just plain straw; it didn't have to be any special kind, but oat straw makes the best filling for a tick.

After it was full they pulled the opening together and sewed it shut. Then, they sewed up and down all through the tick, like upholstery, and tied it off. A straw tick lasted a long time. To make them more comfortable, you turn them over often and use the other side. That keeps it fluffed. They're not very convenient, but it was something to sleep on.

You do the feather bed the same way. We called them ticks too. We made our own feather pillows. If we didn't have a sewing machine, we made them by hand. A lot of people had a sewing machine, but most of the poorer ones didn't.

Odell and me used straw ticks when we lived there in the little- house, but Odell had managed to get a few mattresses by the time we moved out.

# 19

Odell needed someone to help him with the farming. So he asked Charlie Warfford to come stay with us and help him. Charlie was just a boy, no more than twelve years old; he had quit school and was living with his parents in Southmont. His mama probably hated to see him leave home, but it was better for him to work since he had quit school and all.

Odell took half of the little porch that went across the front of the house and made a room out of it and that's where Charlie slept.

Charlie was like a big brother to Foy. He took Foy to school on the school bus the first day he went to school. He took him to school, stayed with him all day, then brought him back home. He took him to school long enough for Foy to learn his way around.

Charlie was mostly help for Odell, not me. We couldn't afford to hire someone to help me. Anything it took to run the house I did it, even if I was pregnant, and I had a baby about every fifteen months. If I couldn't do it, it went undone.

The spring where I got our water was about five hundred feet from the house. So Odell and his daddy and some of JD's friends dug a well closer up to the house. The well had a long pole with a rope and bucket. I would undo the rope and let the pole with the bucket down into the water, then I had to pull the rope back up to pull the bucket out. It still wasn't easy, but it was closer to the house and beat going down to the spring.

The children helped me get the water in some, but they weren't around to help me much. After they got up big enough, Odell took them off to the field to work for him. Odell was a hard worker, but just the jobs he wanted to do.

It was hard, but there were things that I enjoyed about living in the little-house. Everybody in the family used to come and eat—like an open house. Odell's sisters and their families would come. Odell and Will were always together, so Frances and me had a lot of time together. She'd come and visit with Will and bring her two boys, Roy and Dale, and the kids would play and all.

I didn't see Fred much after I got married. While we lived in the Sides house Fred finished high school and went to High Point to work. Then he went into the Air Force. He didn't fly airplanes, he wasn't interested in that. They put him in charge of the supplies. Fred liked the Air Force and made it his life-long career.

The Air Force sent Fred overseas to Germany and different places. In Germany, he met a woman named Rita and they married. When he came back home, he brought Rita out to the house to visit. I liked her.

Fred bought a travel trailer for them to live in and parked it in High Point at Mamas house. So, the next time he was sent overseas Rita lived in the trailer until he came home. Mama and Rita didn't get along too good, so when Fred came back, they moved the travel trailer to the Air Force base in Fayetteville. After that, Fred would always take Rita with him when he was sent somewhere.

Every time Fred came back from a trip overseas, he'd bring me all kinds of pretty things—like beautiful china, porcelain and silver pieces that he got from different places he had been to. My china cabinet in the dining room is full of beautiful things he brought me over the years. Fred and Rita never had any children.

From the back door of Odell's mama's house down to the front of the little-house was a pretty good ways, and it was a slight hill. Sometimes the kids would get out and play on it and ride down it in a little wagon they had to play with.

One day they were taking turns riding and it came Kenneth's turn. So he got in the wagon and got to going down the hill. Well, one of the kids had left a little shovel out there on the hill and when Kenneth got to it, the wagon hit it and turned him over. Kenneth hit his mouth on somethin' nother and cut his lip—deep. We had to take him to the doctor and get it sewed up. He still has the scar from it on his lip if you ever notice.

Another time Charlie and some of the children had gone up to Odell's mama's, and Kenneth decided he was going up there too. I'll say he was three and a-half years old, something like that. To get up there, he had to cross the branch. A plank was laid across the branch right close to the spring and we'd go there and use the plank to cross, and of course when you go across, it would sway some.

The branch was deep at the spring. I guess the water would come up way above your knees if you'd get in it. Well, when Kenneth started across on the plank he stopped, bent over to look in the water at somethin' nother and fell in.

The oil truck was at Odell's mama's and the oil truck man saw Kenneth fall in.

He hollered out, said, "A kid fell in the branch down there!"

Boy, Charlie took off! When he got there, Kenneth had managed to turn over and Charlie pulled him out. If he'd a got strangled Kenneth might a-been in danger. But he was okay. Most of them was tough.

Charlie stayed with us about two years. When he left he went to live with Odell's Uncle George—stayed with him and helped him a little bit. After that, Charlie stayed with Will and Frances for a while and worked in the furniture plant. Then he went into the military service. Later on he married, had a family, and moved out west to Washington. He lives out there yet. He comes in occasionally and he always stops in to see us.

Odell's daddy left his mama. So Odell moved us out from the little-house and in with her so she wouldn't have to be by herself.

Martha

We had lived in the little-house maybe four or five years, something like that. When we moved out, Clara and her family moved in.

I was glad when JD got out from down there. As far as I knew him, he never did nothing but drink and run around. He couldn't get along with anybody. He would get mad at people and do things that were kind of bully like. He always kept a gun around. He kept it loaded and I was always frightened that the kids might get a-hold of it.

One time, for no reason, he got mad at one of his son-in-laws and went after him with the gun. But he didn't find him. I don't know if he would have really shot him or not. A lot of it I think was just a whole lot of show.

JD did some horse trading and cow trading and so on. He did a little bit of everything. And him and his bunch of drinking friends, they'd get together a-messing with the horses and they'd get to drinking and cussing and carrying on. He'd go off with them and stay gone for a while, then he'd come back. This time he went off and stayed.

Martha didn't have much to say about it. It hurt her. Martha lived a pretty hard life, mostly due to JD. He wasn't any help to her. To have some spending money she sold eggs and so on. She was always good to me and good to the children. She was a fine woman.


Glenn and the twins were born after we moved back. Glenn was born June 9, 1937. I named Glenn, I just liked the name Glenn. I don't remember whether I knew a movie actor by the name of Glenn or what. I don't know exactly who, but I just liked the name of Glenn. So, I named him Glenn Edwin. There were fifteen months between Hazel and Glenn.

When I had the twins, all I remember was that I was terrible big. I didn't know I was going to have twins.

It was one hot August day, somewhere about dark. I was fixing my bread and putting it in the pan to set up to rise overnight when my first pain struck me.

Kay was born first.

The woman that was with me said, "Something's wrong. I think there's another one."

I don't remember who was with me, but whoever it was didn't know how to deal with it. I think the cord was wrapped or something.

When Odell found out that she thought another one was on the way he took off like a shot—went to find Dr. Cathell. When the doctor heard what had happened, he took off like a shot coming to the house. Said if he wouldn't a got there when he did, Fay probably would have strangled to death. Dr. Cathell delivered all my babies up through the twins. They made eight. He said he never heard of that many babies from one woman.

The twins were born August 9, 1938. I was twenty-eight years old. I decided on naming them Kay and Fay so they would match. I put Martha with Fay after Odell's mama, and named her Martha Fay. I put Nancy with Kay, and named her Nancy Kay. Nancy was my mama's name. So, they got their grandma's names.

Tommy was only three years old when the twins were born. He turned four that October. Hazel was a little over two and Glenn was just fourteen months. I had the twins and Glenn in diapers. And I don't know if Hazel was fully trained yet.

I cut up old sheets and shirt-tails, just what ever I could get a-hold of to make diapers. People would bring me old sheets and things they couldn't use no more.

I would put the wet diapers in water to soak. If they were soiled, I'd wash them out, put them in water, and let them soak so they wouldn't stain so bad. I had to wash diapers by hand, and I washed about-near every day.

When Kay and Fay were about six weeks old, Center Hill Church gave me a baby shower. I got some pretty things. A lot of people gave me passed down clothes and I sewed what I could.

We managed.

When Kay and Fay were about a year old, I had eight with the measles at one time, and then eight with the chicken pox.

Macks got them first and brought them home to the rest. A little girl in his room at school had been off visiting and come back with the measles and give them to the whole class. Then she got the chicken pox and Macks came home with that. Kay and Fay were broke out so bad with the chicken pox, there was no place on their body you could put your hand down without a bump.

Front row left to right: Kay, Fay and Glenn.
Back row left to right: Hazel, Tommy, Macks, Kenneth and Foy.

Grandma and Grandpa Taylor were not in good health. Grandpa had fluid gathered around his heart that made his feet and legs swell real bad—they called it dropsy. He died June 7, 1940. He was eighty-four. He was born January 6, 1856Grandma Taylor lived maybe four or five months after Grandpa died. She had what you call Alzheimer's. She got so she didn't hardly know what she was doing. They didn't have the rest homes then. She would just go stay with the different ones, but she wasn't satisfied. She died October 14, 1940 at age eighty-two. She was born January 8, 1858.

Foy

Macks

Tommy

Hazel

# 20

Odell bought a Maltese cat, or got a Maltese cat from somebody, or somebody gave it to him, I don't know exactly which. It was a blue gray color.

Of a-night, that cat would go up on the roof and some way or nother he would come down into the attic, then come over the kitchen, and come down *into* the kitchen. There would be cat paw prints all over the table the next morning. I tried to get Odell to stop up the hole he was coming in.

But he'd say, "No, he's got to catch the mice."

Well, that next spring I kept back eggs and set the hens. But I noticed I wasn't having as many biddies as I was supposed to.

I looked out one day, and saw that cat catch a biddy and kill it. I went out there, caught that cat, took it to the woodpile, and chopped its head off.

It was kind of a gentle cat and didn't run from me, I held him

145

tight and that was his last biddy.

When Odell found out, he didn't like it. He wanted it to catch the mice.

That one didn't catch no more.

I said, "The chickens are more important than that cat is."

JD stayed gone for a couple years. Then, every once in a while, he started coming around with one of his drinking and cussing spells, stay long enough to cause trouble, then leave.

I stayed out of the way.

Then, one night he came back to spend the night. During the night, Martha got to crying. So Odell went in and run JD off. I don't know whether he was trying to hurt her or what it was, but it wasn't long after that, that JD come back and stayed all the time.

We moved out. I didn't want to bring up the children around such actions. I don't know exactly how long we lived with Odell's mama that time—maybe two and a half years. But we left and moved up to the Leonard farm on Highway 8—across from where the fish restaurant is now.

The Leonard farmhouse set back off the road some. The front part of the house was one big room that had once been a log cabin. The log cabin part was originally the business office for the Silver Hill Mine. A kitchen was built on to the back of it, and a porch had been enclosed to make two more small rooms.

The house looked more like a barn than a house. Oh, it looked all right from the front, but when you went around to the back, it was just a built up shed. Ice would freeze in buckets in the kitchen. Well, it would do that in Odell's mama's house down there too. We would always put a bucket of water out in the hall to get it of a night if we wanted any. If it was real cold, you couldn't hardly get the dipper out of it.

Doug was born at the Leonard house on March 18<sup>th</sup> 1942. He was born just before World War II broke out, just when America was brought into it. We named him Douglas Odell, Douglas after General Douglas Macarthur, and Odell after his daddy.

Doug made nine children—too many children for Odell to be drafted into the war. They said it cost too much to draft men with that many children.

As usual, after Doug was born the doctor told me to rest in bed for nine days, but I did what I wanted to. When the doctor come back to check on me I was sitting on the side of the bed.

He said, "I thought I told you to stay in bed."

I said, "I *am* in the bed."

Until 1942 I washed clothes by hand on a washboard. When Doug was a baby I told Odell I couldn't wash all that by hand anymore. So he traded a cow for a washing machine—a ringer washer.

Odell would buy, sell, and trade hogs and cows. Whatever he could find he would buy and sell it. Bob Sheets sold washing machines and farmed and dabbled in cows and things. So Odell traded him a cow for a washing machine.

To wash in it, I still had to tote the water a quarter mile from the well. I had to wash daily.

Odell still had his black Ford Roadster, the one he got before we were married. He kept that car 'til we moved up to the Leonard place. He was real proud of that car.

Before we were married Odell had a couple different cars. First he had a Roadster, then he had a Ford Sedan, then he got this Roadster.

One day he was in his first Ford Roadster on Linwood Road going toward the Junior Order Children's Home. When he got to the bridge, he saw Old-man John Lopp Sr. coming toward him from the other side. It was a real narrow bridge. Just one vehicle could cross at a time.

Old-man Lopp had some children in the car with him and he didn't offer to stop before he got to the bridge. Odell said he didn't have time to stop and he couldn't run into old-man Lopp, so he just turned and run off the road to the side.

It didn't hurt the car very bad, but not long after that he traded the Roadster for a Ford sedan. The sedan was closed in—a glassed in car. That all happened while we was dating.

After the Ford Sedan, Odell bought another Ford Roadster and it was one of the fancy ones with a rumble seat. I have a picture of him standing beside of it.

That's the car he had when we got married and that's the car he had when we moved up to the Leonard place.

Years later, sometime in the 1970s, they put that picture of Odell standing beside his Roadster, along with an article about him, and where he grew up in, *The Heritage of Davidson County,* book. Odell was real proud of that.

Old-man Lopp's son, Buck, wanted Odell's Roadster, so Odell traded him the car for a hay baler. Then Odell traded a cow for a truck from Bob Sheets.

Front row from left to right: Hazel, Kay, Fay, Glenn, Kenneth
Back row from left to right: Alma, Doug, Macks, Tommy, Odell, Foy

We lived there at the Leonard farm for two years; then Odell moved us to the southwest side of Lexington to one of the Foster Hankins farms. Foster Hankins owned several large farms around Lexington, maybe four or more.

I never had a choice as to where we moved. Odell picked out what he wanted. If it had a house all right if it didn't all right, and that's where we moved. I never said pea-turkey. I just went along.

149

We moved to the Hankins farm the first day of 1943. That was the last time we moved; we've been here ever since. So that's the story of our moving. I was thirty-three and Odell was thirty-eight. We had been married fourteen years.

The farm had 275 acres of land and two houses, the farmhouse we rented and a smaller one-story rent house across a field from us.

Our house was a big eight room white clapboard two-story with a tin roof. The front entrance had a long hallway, two rooms deep, with a staircase that led upstairs to two small bedrooms. On both ends of the hall were outside doors that went to porches that spread out in both directions. To one side of the hall was a living room and a bedroom, to the other side, two more bedrooms. Beyond the bedrooms was a dining room and a kitchen with a fireplace. The house had electricity, but no sink, no running water. The kitchen had porches front and back, one porch running the length of the house.

It was a beautiful place with lots of tenable land and lots of timber. Sink Inn Road, a dirt road at the time, divided the farm almost in half.

Years before we moved there, the original farmhouse burnt down. 'Course they built it right back. The barn burned down once too. An old tree used to stand beside the barn, I don't know whether it was a pin oak or what, but it was all limbs every which way on it. They said the tree was the cause of the barn burning, maybe lightning. Hankins had a bigger barn built back in its place.

150

I don't remember the barn burning. Somebody that knew the place told us it did; but I know when the house burned. That happened before Odell and me were married. It was when I lived down on South Main Street where the beer plant is now in that house up on the hill. We could see off over here. We could see the blaze and later on, they said that the Hankins farm house burned.

The Foster Hankins Farm

The day we moved, Odell's older brother, George, came to help us. George died at age forty-seven, but he was living when we moved up here to the Hankins farm. All of Odell's brothers and sisters came to help—*all* of them.

We moved on a Saturday. The next day, Sunday, every one of them came in to eat, and they didn't bring one thing. It so happen that I had cooked a big ole chicken the night before, a hen. And other than that, I don't know what else we had. We had enough to eat, I guess.

They just liked to come. To them it was just like home. Odell's brother Will always acted like it was home. They just come on; they never would say when they were coming or nothing. I never had time to fix.

My family visited too, but not like Odell's. Daddy never learned to drive a car, never owned a car, *never.* Nothing but a

Daddy and Mama

horse and wagon or buggy, that's all he ever had. To get anywhere he had to *pick 'em up and set 'em down,* unless he rode with somebody else. So Mama and Daddy only visited when somebody brought them.

Lela and Will would come out to visit and bring their children, Lois, Maxine and Christine.

Julie and Grady brought their four children Ralph, Bucky, Loretta and Doris. Ralph and Bucky used to come some on their own and play ball with the boys.

Virgie and Raymond and their son Bill lived in Fayetteville. So they didn't come to visit much.

Cora married Bill Vance and moved to Atlanta, Georgia.

They would come up on occasion with their kids, Bill Jr., Carol and Wendy.

Flora married Frank Weddington and moved to California. They've lived out there ever since. They had two boys, Butch and Norman, and a girl, Nancy.

Of course Frances and Will were there more than any of the others with their two boys Roy and Dale.

Irvin didn't settle down and get married until he was up in his forties. That was after me and Odell were married and after Mama and Daddy had moved to High Point.

Irvin was too busy running around to get married. He went to Cuba one time. Another time he went to California. He made good money pipefitting and he went where the jobs was, so he went off on these wild goose chases.

When Irvin finally married, he married a woman named Lucille that had already been married and had two children. We didn't get to see them very often because Irvin and Lucille lived in High Point. They never did talk about her first husband or anything.

*P.*

After we got the house cleaned up and kept doing a little something to it, it was pretty good, but it was cold in the winter. In the summer we could leave the doors on both side of the kitchen open and always feel a breeze coming through. An elm tree just outside the kitchen door became a favorite family sitting place, but I never had time to sit out there.

There was a well in the yard near the kitchen porch, but the water wasn't fit to drink; it had a bad taste and went dry a lot. We toted our drinking water from a springhouse down beside the meadow branch.

It was a nice-sized springhouse, about twelve by twenty-four feet divided into two rooms, the springhead room and the milk cooling room. But it was down a steep hill and the kids hated that—carrying water up that steep hill and all. We kept our milk down there.

There was a huge oak tree that sat atop a little bank near the entrance of the springhouse. It leaned over it with big shady limbs and kept it cool in the summertime.

The entrance door was on the springhead side. Then, just inside the door and to the right, was the door to the milk cooling room. The springhouse was built mostly from German siding, except for the springhead side, it was German siding halfway up, then four inch slats about four inches apart the rest of the way. The milk cooling room didn't have any windows and it was dark in there. The darkness made it dangerous for snakes.

The spring itself was a little below ground level and had rocks fixed around it with a cement walking area around the top. The rocks were laid around the spring so that the water could seep between them and run under the wall into the milk cooling room, then into a wooden trough made of oak boards the length of the room. The water in the trough stayed high enough and cool enough that we could set gallon or half-gallon jars of milk in it and they would keep cool 'til the milk was used.

One Christmas recently when the family was gathered together for a holiday meal, my sister Julie's son, Ralph, laughed and told me that as a boy he used to like to sneak down to the springhouse and drink the milk.

In 1943 Lee's wife, Nannie, died of a cerebral hemorrhage. She was only forty-nine years old. Lee never remarried. He lived to be sixty-five years old and died of a heart attack.

Lee and Nannie had fifteen children; their names from the oldest are: Blanche, James, twins Edna and Edward, Madeline, Mary, Louise, Joseph called Joe, Jacob called Jake, Jeanie, Olive, Etta Bell, Evelyn, Betty Lou and Janet.

The girls married names are Blanche Painter, Edna Palmer, Mary Harvey, Louise Kimbrell, Jeanie Byerly, Olive Boyd, Etta Bell Burkhart, Evelyn Mayes, Betty Lou Earwood and Janet Burkholder. Madeline never married.

# 21

When my children were born, the doctors always come to the house and delivered. Then, they began to get the rule pretty strict that you had to go the hospital. So when I knew I was going to have Linda, Odell hunted around and found a doctor that would come to the house, Dr. Andrews.

I asked Odell, "Do you want to name her."

He said, "No, you name her."

I don't know where I got it but I liked the name Linda. So I named her Linda Gail. She was born December 17, 1943, twenty-one months after Doug.

Then, when Linda was twenty-one months old, Foster was born. Dr. Mock delivered Foster. He was born on September 18, 1945.

Odell named him. He named him David after his daddy John David, and Foster after Foster Hankins. We call him Foster.

Foster Hankins gave Foster a fifty-dollar savings bond. Foster was my last baby. That made eleven in all, all born healthy.

Foster laughed one day and said, "You took one look at me and said, *that's enough!*"

I was thirty-five years old when Foster was born. Odell was two weeks from being forty. We had been married sixteen years.

Odell was around when all the children were born, but not too close. Sometimes he would get nauseated and have to leave for a while, but he was somewhere around all the time. I never went to the hospital for any of them.


While I was in the bed after Foster was born, there was a bunch of cream that needed to be churned. We always kept two or three cows for milk and I'd save the cream and churn it and make butter. I mostly churned the butter myself. The children helped churn some and they did all the milking, but I mostly made the butter myself. I had a crank churn and a crock churn. I mostly made it in the crank churn.

I made butter for us and made some to sell. I got twenty-five cents a pound for my butter. I used the money to buy things that was needed. I had quite a few people from around the community coming to buy my butter. Some were regular and some occasional. Some bought milk too. People liked the flavor of whole milk rather than pasteurized.

Having just had Foster, I was supposed to stay in the bed, so I had Odell and the kids to scald the churn out and churn the cream. They got the cream churned all right, and got the butter ready to make out into the butter molds, but nobody could make it out. Nobody knew how to do it. So, Odell put the butter in water and brought it to the bed.

He said, "Tell us how to do this!"

I finally had to sit up on the edge of the bed and make out that butter. Odell was just lost in the kitchen. He didn't know what to do. I was in charge of the house whether I wanted to or was able to or not.

Raising eleven children? Chaos. That's the only thing I can say to describe what it was like. I was the old woman in the shoe. I had so many children I didn't know what to do.

I didn't have any spare time. I didn't have time to worry about what needed to be done. I just did it. I never give it a thought. I knew it had to be done. No wonder I had gray hair. My hair started turning gray when I was in my late twenties. People always thought I was older than I was. Mama's hair turned gray at an early age too, but Daddy's didn't; his was still dark 'til the day he died.

Mealtime was usually hectic. We'd sit down at the table and they'd start to hollering and fussing. If I'd say anything to them, Odell would fuss at me. So, I'd just put out the food and then I'd leave out. Let them manage it whatever way they wanted to. Odell didn't like for me to correct them at the table. He didn't like for me to correct them anytime. To discipline them I'd put them to work;

158

there was always some work or somethin' nother to put them to doing.

I cooked on a wood cook stove. I would cook a big pot of this and a big pan of that. I'd measure out a bucket full of potatoes and peel 'til I thought I had enough. Sometimes I'd peel a gallon or more. 'Til they're cooked up, they don't feed a whole lot.

With pintos, I would fix a great big pot full. We bought pintos by the hundred pound bag. Odell would go get a hundred pounds of beans, a hundred pounds of salt, a hundred pounds of rice and a big bag of potatoes. I don't know how many pounds of potatoes it would be, anyway a big bag, a tow-bag.

With green beans, it would take at least a peck or more. A lot of times he bought them by the baskets. Those baskets that were smaller at the bottom than they were at the top, and they would be full of beans. I don't know how many pounds, maybe fifty pounds. Anyway, we'd eat off them 'til they give out. I don't know how long they lasted; I just cooked. When they run out we got more.

We raised hogs and kept chickens. Odell bought chicks by the hundred. We'd put them in a big box behind the cook stove with a light on them so they would stay warm. We kept them back there 'til they got big enough to turn out.

When I killed and cleaned fryers, I'd clean the heads too. The kids would fuss over the heads—who'd get that—because they'd get the brains, that's all there is on it—just a little brains.

I always have to restrict them to one piece of chicken, 'course not the head or the neck, that was extra because there wasn't nothing on it.

Sometimes when I cooked a big ole chicken, I'd make dumpling out of it. It went further that way. Odell's mama taught me how to make dumplings. Sometimes I made chicken stew and of course I made biscuits, but I never did get the biscuits good like Odell's mama's was. When we lived with her, she did most of the cooking. She always made the biscuits. One day I was in her kitchen stirring up something and singing a song and using the spoon as a timer. She just laughed at me about that—me using the spoon to keep time with my tune.

Odell's mama made what they call potato yeast sourdough bread. She taught me how to make it. You don't have to buy yeast to make sourdough bread so I made that a long time.

Then I learned to make light bread. I learned to make it all by myself. The light bread had to have yeast, so Odell bought yeast at the store so I could make it.

Mama had a flour chest. She gave it to me to store my flour in. Daddy's uncle made the flour chest for Mama while we were living in the backwoods. He lived down in Silver Hill and used to make furniture. The chest had two sides, a big side for storing flour and a smaller side for cornmeal. The flour side was big enough to hold a hundred pounds of flour.

Every evening I would get flour out of the chest and make light bread. I'd let the dough set over night to rise. The next morning I'd punch it down and make it out into biscuits so it would rise and be ready 'til dinnertime. I always kept another batch coming on for the next meal. What bread was left from supper, we ate for breakfast the next morning. When the flour got low, Odell would take a couple bags of wheat to the mill and trade it for flour.

Sometimes Odell killed cows to sell or trade to local grocery stores; you could do that then. He'd keep enough for the family to eat on so we always had plenty. Then he'd sell some. One store would take half a cow and another store the rest. Sometimes one store would take a whole one.

When Odell wanted to kill a cow he'd say, "Come out here Alma and help me skin this cow."

If a baby was asleep in the house, I'd have to go and leave them a-sleeping.

Odell would say, "Come on, they'll be all right."

Or when he had cotton planted in the big field between our house and Hankins' little rent house, he would say, "Come on and hoe cotton," and whatever child was little I had to leave them in the house and go hoe cotton. I was scared to death. I would hoe a little bit and look back toward the house.

I don't remember if it was Foster or Doug, but when they was a baby, I had them in a baby crib that had metal rods about six inches apart around the bed, and if you pushed on them, they'd give.

Well, the baby wiggled and got its body through two of the rods, but its head didn't go through. I found it hanging like that. It was all right, but from then on, 'til they got big enough to get up by themselves, I always put something around the bed to keep them from coming through. The Lord gave them to us and gave us a little bit of sense to take care of them, but the Lord took care of them too.

Hazel with her daddy

Doug

Foster

Hazel

Kay

Fay

Glenn

Doug

Foster

163

# 22

For years I didn't go to church anywhere. We didn't have one close by, Odell wouldn't go and I had no way to go by myself.

While we lived in the Sides house I walked to Center Hill Baptist church some. I joined Center Hill.

When we moved up here to the Hankins farm there wasn't any churches close around 'til Meadowview Presbyterian Church was formed.

The children were going to Robbins School at the time. The principal, Mrs. Reed, would always, on Monday mornings, she'd always ask the children to raise their hand if they went to church that Sunday. She got to noticing that a certain group never went to church. That was the ones from down here in our area.

So she got to investigating and she had Sarah Little from First Presbyterian Church up town to look into it. I guess you could call

Sarah a home missionary or church establisher. Sarah came around our neighborhood to all the homes to ask if they would go to church if one was established nearby. Most of them said yes.

So they got to looking around for a place to meet and found an old abandoned building on Highway 29, behind where the Highway Patrol station is now. It had first been built for a filling station; then later on, some separate small cottages were built out from it and rented out as a motel.

To make us a meeting place, they took the filling station part and tore the partitions out and made it like an auditorium for us to meet in.

On a Sunday evening in November of 1944 we had our first church meeting. Forty some people came. About near every family on what we called, *the hill*, on Sink Inn Road, came to that first church meeting in the old filling station.

A lot of others that lived further out came too. We were all thrilled about it. We met there for church services for about three or four years. I started as a charter member. Odell didn't attend.

We kept wanting to build a church, so finally a Sink man sold us land on Beethoven Avenue, up behind *the hill* off Sink Circle, and we built our church building there.

First Presbyterian Church was still heading off everything, and when we got our building finished and went in, they elected officers and established it as Meadowview Presbyterian Church, a part of the Southern Presbyterian Church.

While we were getting our start, Second Presbyterian Church

on Cotton Grove Road was doing the same thing for Fairmont Presbyterian Church.

Fairmont got its start in the home of one of its members. They met there until they built their church down on Cotton Grove Road near the forks of Cotton Grove and Fairview Drive. They finished their church just before we did.

Rev. Bill Link came and serviced both churches for us as pastor. He preached at Meadowview and Fairmont for three or four years.

At first, we didn't have anything for the children, so First Presbyterian sent Mildred Snyder, a home missionary, to come in and go around through the neighborhood to teach the children in the yards and start youth groups and things like that. Mildred was a young girl from Virginia, just out of college. She started youth groups, kept them going, and started the *Women In The Church* and *Circle* groups for the ladies.

The pastor from First Presbyterian Church brought Mildred to the house one day to introduce her to me. I asked them in. The pastor had been to the house several times before and knew my circumstances.

He looked at Mildred and told her to, "Just wait out here." 'cause he knew my house was a mess.

I didn't blame him. I was thankful for it.

Before Meadowview was started it was hard for me to make acquaintance with other women because I didn't get out much. I had gone to the parent teacher meetings at the schools when I could get there, but that was very seldom because I didn't have nobody to take me. Now I had a church close enough that the kids and me could walk to it. Sometimes, if it was rainy or bad, Odell would take us to church in the truck. But most of the time he was gone here and yonder down to his mama's. I told the children the truck didn't know anywhere to go but to the home place. Odell never took the children on any trips. Odell and me never went on a trip together.

He went on a trip one time. He went up somewhere towards West Jefferson, North Carolina with Mr. Dillard, a friend of his. They planned on staying three or four days. Came back the next day. He didn't ever go off again. He didn't like to go to nobody's house but his own people.


The church meant a lot to me. The church was my social life. It meant a lot that I could go regular every Sunday. Getting to know other women through the Circles and Women in the Church gave me a view on the outside. It was nice.

Sometimes the women would meet with churches in Mocksville or Winston-Salem, or other Presbyterian churches here in town. We would all ride together and have fun that way. Zelma Garrett was elected as our president. She was a good leader.

Edna Prevette lived on *the hill* and she became my close friend. I got to know Mary Clemmer through Edna. My children had played with Mary's children, Jack, Louise and Nancy, but I didn't know Mary until Edna introduced us. I got to know Mary Layton, Gloria Prevette and Mozell Walser. I got to know the Curry's after they moved on *the hill* and started coming to church. They became good workers.

Foster was the first baby of the church. The church wasn't established yet when he was born, it was still a mission, but he was the first baby. The church started in November and Foster was born the next September. Mary Clemmer's little boy that died, he would have been the first one, but Foster was the first one. I don't know if they kept records about that.

# 23

We had been living on the Hankins farm about four years when Mr. Hankins started coming to Odell saying, "Sonny, let me sell you this place."

Odell would say, "No, I can't buy it. I don't have that kind of money."

Hankins told him, says, "You can make good money growing corn."

Odell would just turn his ear. He wanted the farm, but he didn't think he could manage to pay for it and all, but Mr. Hankins just kept on talking to him. Mr. Hankins liked Odell because he was a hard worker.

One day a colored man that worked on one of Mr. Hankins other farms saw Odell, he says, "You better buy that farm," Says, "Yes you can."

So, it went on like that.

Odell talked to me about buying the Hankins farm and I told him if he thought he could make it, well go ahead. He was real good with money. Odell had been doing custom farming work for other people and made more doing that than he could working at public work. Then besides that, he would buy up cows and kill them and sell them and made two or three times more than what he paid for them. He was doing all right.

Mr. Hankins kept a-wanting Odell to pay down on the place and row crop. Odell wasn't about to do that. He knew he couldn't pay for the place like that, but Mr. Hankins kept on. So finally, Odell had managed to save enough money to make a three thousand dollar down payment, and he went ahead and paid down on it. He got a mortgage for the rest. The deal included the house we were living in, the rent house, and 275 acres of land.

I don't remember exactly what the sale price was for the farm, but Mr. Hankins says, "Sonny, you're a-gittin' a bargain."

Now, Odell could farm the land any way he wanted to, and farm in a much bigger way. He wouldn't have to go off hunting for other land to farm, but he did anyway. He worked hard.

Having the farm to pay for and eleven kids to feed and raise didn't seem to worry Odell, I didn't say it didn't worry me though. But the Lord provided.

Before we bought the farm, Hankins had cut some of the timber off the place. Odell had them come back in and cut the rest. He got enough money from that to make a pretty good payment on it.

Foy

Macks

Glenn

Kenneth

Tommy

He sold hay and straw that he baled off other farmers fields. They would give it to him to bale just to get it off their fields. Sometime they asked a little bit for it, but not much.

When Odell raised wheat, he'd combine his and combine other peoples too. That's the way he paid for his farm equipment. He'd buy hogs and take them to the hog market and make a little money like that. He got good at figuring what they'd bring.

Our boys worked and helped Odell in the field. Everybody used to brag about how hard our boys worked. All the way down to Foster they worked in the field. It was hard on the kids 'cause every time they would get a holiday from school Odell would have a job already picked out for them to do. They didn't get to be with their buddies or nothing. It irked them.

Macks run into some mighty close places in the field. Once he almost got baled up in the hay baler. He was down in the baler cleaning it out and somebody started it up. A colored man was working up above Macks and he had great long arms. He just reached down and picked Macks right out. It was a miracle that he was up there. If there were other close times, they didn't tell me about those and I'm sure there probably were.

Odell finally had a deep well punched and run water into the house for me. They punched one hole, got way down, and broke the bit off. They tried every way they could to get that bit out but

172

couldn't. So, they decided to dynamite it to see if that would get it out—didn't do a thing. That bit is over there in the ground yet. I don't know how many—50, 60, 80 feet—I don't know how many feet down it is. They just put a disk over the top of the hole, moved over about thirty foot and punched another hole. That one worked. That well is still in use.

For a kitchen sink, Odell used one that somebody had discarded. Some of them found it when they were out somewhere and brought it home. It was in fairly good condition so Odell put it up in the kitchen and that's what we used. I guess it was pretty good; it's still in use. It's been there more than fifty years.

The kids were sure glad they didn't have to haul water up from the springhouse anymore.


Foster was a pretty good size boy when we got a refrigerator. The first refrigerator we had was one that used to be in the Junior Order Children's Home. It was one they bought when they first opened up. A man that worked there bought it from them during the depression or during the war—some time along there.

He was wanting to get rid of it, so Odell traded him a cow or a pig or somethin' nother for it. Odell was a trader. He was a good trader. Give him a cow or a pig and he knew what to do with it.

We still have that refrigerator out on the back porch of the old farmhouse.

The first we knew they were coming through the farm with Interstate Highway 85 Bypass was when we saw them out there surveying. That was in the late forties. Oh, there was talk about them going down Michael's Creek, but they figured that was too expensive. Then there was talk about it going somewhere else. But finally it was decided that it would come right through our farm. It cut the property nearly in half. It was very disappointing.

Odell and his straw stack

Since we hadn't finished paying for the farm yet and due to not having the deed and all Odell just had to agree to what the state offered for the land. He didn't get much. Our neighbor got more for her swampland and all than we got for our good farmland. While they were building the highway, they wanted straw to put on the banks to keep them from washing away. So Odell sold straw to them. He had a pile of baled up straw in the barnyard almost as big as the barn. He sold most of it to them.

With what money he got from the state and from the straw, Odell had enough money to get the land into his name. Then he was all right.

# 24

The Grimes, that lived south of town in that great big white two-story house near the county airport, had a mare pony named Scout. She was white with brown patches. Their boy had got too big for the pony and they were wanting to get rid of it. I'm not sure whether they gave it to Odell or sold it to him, anyway Odell got it.

Scout was old when we got her, and we had her for more than twenty-five years. She was special to us, a family pet. The kids had a good time with Scout. We had a yard full of children all the time wanting to ride. Frances Alley, my distant

Odell with Scout and her colt Ginger

cousin's daughter, lived nearby. She was friends with Hazel, and

175

Hazel

her sister, Vivian, was about the same age as Kay and Fay. So, Frances and Vivian would come over to ride.

Frances would just get out there and look Scout straight in the eye and say, "Now you just behave."

Scout would just stare back.

We used to laugh at how much sense Scout had and how Frances wasn't one bit afraid of her.

Archie Sink, a good friend of Odell's since childhood, got a-hold of a banker pony, a male pony, named Dan. He was from the wild horses of the outer banks of North Carolina.

Archie had a farm in Linwood and owned a farm implement store. Odell bought all his farming equipment from Archie and did some work on his farm for him, like haymaking and things like that.

Archie decided he didn't want the pony anymore so he gave it to Odell. We have pictures of Odell and Will riding Dan and Scout. They'd just ride them bare back with their legs hanging down—almost to the ground.

Odell learned to ride horses as a boy. Will and Odell would ride their daddy's workhorses to the school house and back. Odell could stand up on their back and ride.

Odell on Dan & Will on Scout

Scout had a colt by Dan, a mare colt. They named her Ginger

176

because of her reddish coat. Next came Boots, a bay with black legs.

I was mopping the floors one Saturday morning when Dr. Morgan comes out to the house with his little girl to ride the ponies. The house had plain wood floors; so to clean them I'd just pour a bucket of water on the floor and mop it with lye soap. The floors had little holes bored in them so the water could run out under the house. What water didn't run out, I'd sweep out the door with the broom and dry up the rest with the mop. That's the way I cleaned the floors before we got the linoleum put down.

Everybody was gone that morning but me. And when Dr. Morgan came, there I was with a broom in my hand sweeping water out the door onto the porch.

Dr. Morgan stood there and looked at me.

Then he said, "I'll come back another time."

I told him, "Well, you'll have to, 'cause I don't have anything to do with the ponies."

That was embarrassing to me and I know it was embarrassing to him. I bet he thought, "What kind of people are them?"

I did a lot of my cleaning with lye soap. I made my own in a big iron wash pot in the yard. I took pork fat and meat skins, put them in the pot over a fire and cooked 'em out. Then I put in *Red Devil Lye* that I bought at the grocery store. I kept a fire under it and stirred it 'til it made a soap. Sometimes I put perfume in it to flavor it—that didn't take the strongness out of it. I used the lye soap to clean floors, clothes, and most anything else that needed cleaning.

Linda

All of the girls were tomboys, but I guess Linda was the most active child of all. She just lived on the horses. When we got the ponies, she was the first one to ride. She would ride anything she could get on.

A little horse show got started out here in the Reeds community at the Ray Craver place. Some of them built up a little neighborhood horse club out there and named it the *Happy Hill Saddle Club.*

Odell and some of them got started going to the horse shows, and I'd go with them just to watch and to see the other people. They had the barrel races and the egg races and things like that. Linda rode a horse of Archie's named Silver in the races. He was real fast. She showed a walking horse named Roy for somebody too.

One day Odell and Archie brought home a wild horse. He was a gelding named Sargo from the June Little farm—never been handled, never been rode. His daddy was a registered horse from Kentucky.

It took three men to get Sargo in his stall. Odell warned the kids to stay away from him. But when nobody was around Linda and Doug would go out to the barn and pet him. When he got used to them they started putting saddles on him. They broke him like that.

Linda trained Sargo for the horse shows and won a lot of trophies with him, some good trophies. Odell got a palomino colt from somewhere down in Denton. He was real pretty. Odell named him Golden Captain. He raised him as a stallion and worked with him and trained him for the shows. He won some big trophies with him.

Odell loved that horse more than he loved me.

Linda on Sargo

Linda on Roy

Golden Captain

All the kids just loved to ride the horses, especially the girls. They would ride out off through the woods, and I wouldn't know where they were. I'd just have to wait 'til they got back. I didn't know whether they were all right, whether the horses had throwed them off or what. They got bruised up now and then, but the Lord was taking care of them.

Fay and Kay

A whole bunch of times, on Sundays, they would get together with the people from the saddle club and go riding all around the countryside.

I wished that I could ride, but I never had time to learn. The only time I was on a horse was when I was small. When I rode my daddy's workhorses back from the field or something like that, no pleasure riding. One day Linda and Kay and Fay ask me to go horseback riding with them. Said they wanted to put me on a horse. Said they were going to teach me how to ride. So I went along.

Not being around horses since I was a child, I didn't know how or what to do to handle it or make it listen or nothing.

At first we walked along at a slow pace. Then, some way another their horses got to running, so my horse started running too. It scared me. I didn't know how to control it to get it stopped. Linda got up beside me, got it stopped, and took me back to the barn. They never put me on a horse again.

# 25

One of our pigs had two babies. She stepped on them when they were born and cut a little gash in the shoulder of one; so Odell brought them to the house 'til that healed up. Then, when he took them back, the mama, she wouldn't have them. So we raised them in the kitchen in a box behind the woodstove. The kids fed them on the bottle.

Them pigs were the awfulest things. They wouldn't stay in their box; they'd climb out and run around the kitchen. So as soon as we could, we turned them out. After that, the kids would go to the door and sit on the steps with the bottle and feed them. Kay and Fay were the ones that mostly tended to them.

When they got up a little bigger, if nobody was there when they wanted the bottle they'd start clawing on the screen. They kept tearing out the screen and tearing out the screen. Just as quick as they got six weeks old Odell sold them.

Kay and Fay cried. So Archie Sink gave them two little lambs from his farm that the mama wouldn't have. Kay and Fay raised the lambs on the bottle too. They'd bring them in their bedroom at night and put them in a box, then take them back to the barn the next morning.

Odell got tired of them being in the house, so he gave them back to Archie.

Kay and Fay

When the children were born, we always gave the names to the doctor and they always sent them in.

When Tommy was in high school, he wanted to play ball and had to have his birth certificate. When he went to the courthouse to get it they said, "We don't have it. We just have, a baby boy." no name was ever turned in.

We named him Thomas Claude, but we always called him Tommy and he went ahead and gave it Tommy instead of Thomas. So, that was all right too.

When Tommy was a little older, he had problems breathing. The doctor had the lung X-rays done for TB. They come back clear. Well, he kept getting sick, couldn't breath, and the doctor wanted more tests of it. So they sent him to Winston-Salem to

183

have X-rays made. Tommy had to go back again and they took bigger X-rays or something. Anyway, they found a tumor on his lung.

Tommy

They wanted him to have the surgery to remove it, so he went on and had it done. The doctor said the tumor was as big as a grapefruit. They said if he had fell and that thing would of busted, well that would a-been it.

He got along just fine. I don't think he's had any problems with it since. If they hadn't found it I don't know what it might have turned into.

The other kids were healthy, no problems, except for an accident now and then.

The boys would go out with Edna's husband, Simon Prevette, and ramble around through the woods and swing on grapevines. They had one they liked to swing on up above the springhouse. Tommy was swinging on it and fell and broke his arm.

He came in toting his arm and said, "I think I broke my arm."

He wasn't crying or nothing, just, "I think I broke my arm."

Glenn broke his arm. When we moved here to the farm it came with a horse named Nell, a mule named Jack. They were kept down in the lower pasture near the springhouse. When the grass in the yard got high Odell would bring them up into the yard to eat it down.

Odell had put them in the yard that day and they were running around all over it. Glenn was outside on the porch watching them. He wasn't but seven or eight years old. Nell and Jack were running around so wild that he was afraid to get down off the porch into the yard; afraid they would run over him. The house wasn't underpinned; just open underneath. It was just a low porch,

Glenn

two and a half to three foot high. So Glenn laid down on his belly on the porch and bent a-way over so he could look through under the house and see them running on the other side. He stretched over a little bit too far trying to see and got over balanced and fell off the porch. The fall broke his left arm. It wasn't serious.

Doug, he goes out on the other porch and takes a chair, and instead of setting it up straight to sit in it, he turned it upside down and propped it up against the wall. Then he climbed up on it. It slipped and slid down the wall and he fell and broke his arm.

When Doug was in high school he was in the gym playing, and they had some kind of net; I don't know what it was for. But they was trying to jump over it.

Doug jumped over it; then went back to try to jump over it again. That time he flopped down and broke his arm. That night

185

he had to stay in the hospital. I guess it was because he was at school and it was a school accident. The school paid for it.

When the children were small the doctor would say to give them cod liver oil. All children were supposed to get cod liver oil. It was good for the bones—rickets. We were told if they didn't get a certain kind of vitamin they'd get the rickets. I gave them cod liver oil daily. I don't remember whether I gave them a teaspoon or a tablespoon. The doctor prescribed it. I had the awfulest time giving them cod liver oil. It tastes so bad they didn't want to take it. So, I finally put it in orange juice to get them to take it. Tommy says to this day he can't stand orange juice.

At times, as the children were growing up, neighbors would come and ask me what to do about this and that when someone was sick. All I could tell them was what had worked for me, and this, that and the other and try to think sensible.

One of the things that I wanted to do as a girl that I didn't get to do was; I always wanted to be a nurse. But I quit school. I didn't even get a grammar grade education so that knocked that out. The one thing I regret most is quitting school. I always loved to go to school. Mama should have made me go on to school. Mama didn't have much education, and they needed me to work. Sometimes I just wonder if I had a-went on and finished high school what I would have been. It wasn't meant to be.

# 26

The children kept fussing at Odell to get rid of the wood cook stove and get an electric stove, so he finally got me one. Kay and Fay were big girls by that time.

He got it in the spring. He bought it; he didn't trade for that. It made a lot of difference in the kitchen being cool or hot. In the summer time, with the woodstove, it took a long time to get the heat out of the kitchen.

Kay and Fay milking

So, then I had a refrigerator, an electric stove and running water. That was wonderful.

Next, Odell bought a freezer. He bought it from the *50-50 Super Market* on Cotton Grove road. We set it on the back porch.

One day a van stopped out in the yard and a man come up to the door and said, "I got a flat tire," said, "I got my van loaded down with candy. Can I leave it here; can you all use it?"

I didn't know what to say.

"I'm just giving it to you," he said, "you don't have to pay nothing."

It was candy he'd picked up at the stores that had got old and they wasn't selling any longer.

I said, "Yeah, I guess so."

He unloaded it and put all of it in that freezer. We kept it out there and if anybody wanted candy they'd go out there and raise the lid and get them candy.

Foster would go eat it so much 'til it caused a kidney problem and we had to take him to the doctor. I think that was the start of his diabetes. That's what I've always thought.

The doctor gave him medicine and he got all right, but he wouldn't stop eating. He ate everything he wanted and he finally got diabetes. All of them got fat. It was this expensive candy.

If he had a broke down and brought some meat that would have been nice. The candy was too dangerous.


One day a dump truck came up to the house and the man said, "I've got a load of sand rock on my truck and I got a flat tire." Said, "I can't fix it 'til I get the sand rock off. Can I dump it here?"

I looked at him and he said, "It won't cost you nothing. It's

188

free."

I said, "Okay,"

So he dumped the load of sand rock out there near the barn.

When Odell got home he said, "What's that sand rock doing out there? I haven't ordered any sand rock."

I said, "No, a man had a flat tire and left it out there."

Odell didn't know what to say.


One time a helicopter came over and passed over a big tree in the field and landed in the pasture. We ran out to see what was going on and met some men coming up toward the house. They said they'd run out of gas. They were from down east somewhere.

The airport was just a few miles away, so I told them where it was. They decided to go on to the airport. We stood there and watched them take off. It was exciting. A few exciting things happened.

Odell and me put all of the children through high school. When Hazel finished school she decided she wanted to go into nursing, a lot of the girls were going into nursing. So she went to the Baptist Hospital in Winston-Salem to train. She made it

Hazel in her nurse's uniform

'til Christmas. That's when they got to teaching them how to give

189

the shots—use the hypodermic needle. That was the end of that. She said she didn't want that.

Foster

Foster went to Catawba College one year. I don't think any of the rest of them went to college at all until later. What they got they took some courses later.

While Hazel was going to nurses training, Odell put a bathroom in the house with a shower. I think Hazel talked him into it, but Odell was a-wanting a toilet anyway. I think he got tired of going down the path.

They never asked us when they started getting married. Foy was the first to marry. He married Shirley Bishop. They got married at the Bishop's house. That and Doug's was the only public weddings. Some of them got married at the preacher's house. Tommy and Loretta were married in High Point. Some of them went to South Carolina and I don't know where some of them got married. The only two I was at was Foy's and Doug's.

Foy married Shirley Bishop, Macks married Virginia (Tootsie) Bean, Kenneth married Clorie Bivens, Tommy married Loretta Hedrick and Hazel married Homer Shipwash. Glenn married Nancy Blankenship, Kay married James Atwell, Fay married Lonnie Michael, Doug married Pat Wallace, Linda married Sam Garwood, and Foster married Lana Vestal.

Hazel and Homer divorced. Hazel remarried to Bill

Cockerham.

I think I was in my late forties when my first grandchild was born, a girl. I was very proud to be a grandmother. She was Foy and Shirley's first child. They named her Judy.

I can remember going out in the yard carrying Judy and bragging to a visitor, "See! Here's my first grandchild!"

After Judy, came Bradley, then Carol, Hazel and Homer's daughter. Then, after that, they just kept coming. Now I have over seventy grandchildren, great grandchildren and great-great grandchildren, I love them all.

In 1958 Odell's mama had a stroke that made her so she couldn't talk. She was in the Lexington Hospital for nearly a month. They said they couldn't keep her anymore; so we had to put her in a rest home up close to Winston-Salem. She stayed in the rest home from May 'til August. She never did get so she could talk or say anything.

Foy and Shirley and me were up there visiting her one night and she kept motioning and motioning and grunting and so on.

Foy said, "Grandma what do you want."

She pulled him down toward her.

Foy said, "Do you want to say something,"

She whispered real faintly, "yeah."

He gave her a pencil and paper. She was left-handed and the

stroke had affected her left side, so she had to write with her right hand. She was writing like we would with our left hand.

Foy held the paper for her to write and she wrote, *HOME*.

JD and Martha

The next week, she died. I think she had another stroke. That was in August. She was eighty-six. She lived from November 15, 1872 to August 20, 1958.

JD died the next year. He lived nine months after Martha died, no longer. Will took care of him, so I don't know what he died of. Heart failure probably. That's what they put on most of them. He lived from November 26, 1877 'til May 26, 1959. He was eighty-one.

My daddy died November 1, 1959. He lived to be 82 years old. He was born September 12, 1877. He died of uremia. His kidneys give out and he died with a bleeding ulcer. He got to bleeding one night and got sicker and sicker. Mama called some of us and we went over there to try to help her.

They took him on to the hospital and he never came out. He was a sick man. The doctors drew fluid from him. I don't know whether he ever got so he knew anyone after that. He never did ever fully regain his strength.

I was standing at the door of his room when he died. His stomach was going up and down, up and down.

He stopped breathing and one of the sweetest expressions came on his face, as if to say, "Thank you Lord." 'Course he couldn't say anything, but you could think that, from his expression. He was the only one I ever saw pass on.

Daddy died the day after Halloween. Mama said she was scared to death that someone was going to come knocking on the door for trick or treat while he was in the hospital. I guess the mothers controlled them, because nobody never come.

Mama lived twelve years after Daddy died. She lived to be 92. She died in the rest home of a stroke. She was sick about a week. After she got sick she didn't know anybody. She knew when

Nancy Caroline and Stephen Harris Cross

we came in the room, but she couldn't place whether we were her children or not. She died April 3, 1972. She was born July 29, 1879.

# 27

In my late 50s I decided I wanted to do public work again for a while, so I went to work at a little hosiery mill, Irving Hosiery Mill, about three miles from the house. That was after Linda had finished high school.

Odell would take me over there and he was supposed to come get me of an evening. One evening he didn't come get me. So, I took off walking, and I walked all the way home. Got home, he wasn't there.

He come in, said, "How'd you get home?"

"I walked! Where was you at?"

"I was out here working around with somebody."

I had a crying spell and that was the last of it that I worked.

I never even thought about my years until the day I turned sixty.

I got to thinking, why goodness, I'm ancient.

I never thought about the others.

It was around about that time that I got interested in the Agricultural Extension Homemakers Clubs. For years I'd wanted to join, but I never had a way to the meetings.

One day Frances was fussing, says, "I haven't got anything to do. I just sit around here."

I said, "Well, why don't we join the homemakers group."

She said, "What's that."

I explained it to her, how they meet together and have speakers to talk to us about all kinds of things to do with the home; so we got to going together to the meetings. I don't remember how we went, 'cause she wasn't driving then. Anyway, Frances liked it, and she didn't like it.

Our group was making plans to go to Raleigh to the fair. We hadn't officially joined yet, but you didn't have to be a member to go. It didn't cost much, about five dollars, so we went with them.

Frances liked that all right. She went to one or two more meetings, then one day I was going on about the magazine the homemakers put out, talking about how they had put in something about the club we were going to, and she said, "Who wants to read that stuff? I want to do something, not just read it." So, she just quit.

I stayed with it and joined. I got to the meetings the best way I could.

The homemakers club planned trips to different places. Trips to places around North Carolina, and trips to other states. Every now and they planned trips to other countries. I went with them most every time they went somewhere. I got most of my money to go doing baby-sitting for Hazel and Linda. Hazel had four children, Carol, Skip, Sherrie and Jill and Linda had Lynn.

Linda paid me for keeping Lynn. Jill was there a whole lot and Hazel was paying me something for that. I didn't charge them anything, but that was how I was getting my money to go on my trips. On the big ones, Odell would give me a little bit.

I've been in all the seaboard states from Maine to Florida. 'Been to California, 'been to Missouri and South Dakota. I've been to Holland and all around over there.

I went with the homemakers club to Europe. One day a dozen of us women rode on the train into Paris, France. My friend Geneva Harrelson was with us.

She said, "I came all the way to Paris, France to ride on a train."

It was the first time she had ever rode on a train.

We went to Amsterdam and up the Rhine River into Germany. We came back on a boat. It was a real nice trip. The travel was enjoyable and educational.

I didn't buy souvenirs. That's just a waste of time. All my pretty dishes and things from other countries—that's what Fred and Rita brought me.

# 28

It must have been the early part of the seventies when we moved out of the farmhouse. Hazel and Homer built a white brick house on the backside of the farm on Pinetop Road. After their divorce Hazel wanted to sell it. Odell had always wanted a nice brick home so I urged him to buy it and he went ahead and bought it. Odell had everything painted. He was very proud of it. He even washed all the doorknobs.

I thinks, "Oh boy, now I'm going to have some help."

The house had electric ceiling heat and after we moved in, Odell laughed and said, "I'm not going to cut no more firewood. I'm not going to buy no more oil. I'm just going to sit back and soak up the heat from the electric ceiling."

That lasted one month and he was through with that. The electric ceiling heat didn't put out enough heat to suit him. He cut wood and built fires in the fireplace in the living room for a little while, but that wouldn't heat the whole house, so he got him a woodstove and set it in the fireplace on the raised hearth. He let the fire coals roll out all over the rug and burned holes in it.

Then it got so it hurt his back to try to carry the wood and all, so he closed up the fireplace and replaced the woodstove with a gas heater. The gas heater wasn't vented and smelled so bad. I didn't like it.

Foy came one day and said, "You need to get rid of that thing. It's going to kill you."

I was drawing money from social security, and I had Tommy to get us a new gas stove at the gas company where he worked. It was vented and it didn't smell. Odell grumbled a little bit, but he liked it.

Odell didn't want central air conditioning either, but I went ahead anyway and got it done. He really enjoyed that.

Odell and Alma in their new home

In 1982 the World's Fair came to Knoxville, Tennessee. I went to it with the homemakers club. Someone told Odell the fair had the Chinese wall. Well, they had the imitation of it, yeah. They might have had just one piece that they claimed was from China.

Odell said, "Bring me a piece of China back."

What they had was just what you'd buy in any store. So, I brought him a piece. It ain't nothing.

Odell wouldn't go anywhere. I think he was too embarrassed or I don't know exactly what. He didn't like to be in a crowd or anything. Anybody he knew he was all right, but in a crowd he would just clam up. He said it gave him a headache. I think the nervousness of being in a crowd made him have a headache.

He wouldn't even go out with Fred and Rita when they came to visit. That always puzzled me. But he could go over here to the farmers livestock market and jabber all evening and nothing, or to a horse show and never have the headache. Anything like going to church, "My head hurts." It's always been odd to me.

When he was a boy, he would go to hotdog places and things like that. I don't know about going to a restaurant, but he wouldn't go with a girl, or not with me.

I guess it's just been since he moved over here to the new house that he would get out and go anywhere. If the kids would get around him and kid him, well then he would go.

He did enjoy running the golf driving range though. Before

they divorced, Hazel and Homer built *Pinetop Golf Driving Range* in the big field across Interstate Highway 85 Bypass from the farmhouse. They ran it for a couple years and decided they didn't want it any more, so Odell bought the equipment from them and ran it himself.

Odell never played golf in his life, but he really enjoyed running the driving range. It kept him busy. People would come out from all over town to hit balls.

When I was about 68 years old, Glenn's wife, Nancy, offered to teach me how to drive a car. After her daddy died Nancy taught her mother to drive. So when Mrs. Blankenship got her license, Nancy offered to teach me. I had never driven a car.

I told Odell, says, "I'm going to get my driving license."

He said, "Huh, you won't get them."

That made me more determined.

I needed to get my driving permit first, so I got a book and studied the driving rules.

I wasn't afraid when I took my test. I don't know why. I wasn't a bit afraid. I passed the test the first time.

Then, for weeks Nancy and me drove all over the country-side so I could get comfortable driving the car.

Nancy knew the driving route the examiner took for the driving licenses test from teaching her girls and her mother to drive, so one afternoon we practiced all the turns until I got them down perfect. She told me I was ready, so we went right then and I took my driving test.

I passed.

When I come home, I took my driving license and placed them down in front of Odell.

He said, "What do you want?"

I said, "Here's my driving license."

He said, "You didn't get them."

I said, "Here they are!"

He would never ride with me. He never did ride with me. He never did ride with me under the wheel. I don't care. I drove his food over to the driving range for him though. I went over there and stayed some for him and run the driving range when he wanted to come home and rest, but he didn't trust me at it. He'd always question me about it after he came back. He thought I didn't know how to do nothing.

# 29

Odell had always wanted a motor home, so he bought one. He would take the motor home over to the driving range and sit in it. He took it over there one day, got in there and shut the door and went to sleep. I think it was spring or summer I don't know which, anyway it got hot in there.

When he woke up he couldn't see, and he couldn't hardly walk. He couldn't tell what things were and so on. When he did get out of the motor home, he went into the driving range building and sat there 'til he got to feeling a little better. Macks came by and saw that something was wrong and drove him on home.

By us insisting, he went to the doctor. The doctor couldn't find anything. He thought it was a heat stroke or something, and he told him not to drive anymore.

You might as well a-said drink water. He would drive wherever he wanted to drive.

Then one day him and Will had been down to the family home place picking up pears, and his back got to hurting him. So, finally he went to the doctor about that. The doctor said it was arthritis or somethin' nother.

Then his kidneys got to bothering him. He couldn't pass water too good. He went to the doctor and the doctor did a test and could feel a little knot. He sent Odell on to the hospital in Winston-Salem for more tests. They put him through the scanner and all that.

Over there, they said it was cancer. They said it was his prostate. 'Course he didn't want to have nothin' done. They wanted him to take the radiation but he didn't want to.

The doctors finally persuaded him to have the radiation. He had thirty-six treatments of that. Once or twice the treatment made a little red place where they would do it.

Odell kept having problems, and I don't know what all they did to decide it, but they decided that he had bone cancer. By that time there wasn't anything could be done for him. They did do the prostate surgery. That was to keep the pain down—keep it from hurting him so bad. I think it must of helped because he never did go on about the pain. He didn't get any better though. As far along as it was I don't think the chemo would have helped.

We couldn't get Odell to go to bed. He said he felt shut off back in the bedroom. He'd sit in the living room in his recliner. He slept in the living room in the recliner. He just sat there and slept all the time.

It got so he couldn't hardly get out of the chair when he needed to, so finally they persuaded him to go to his bedroom. He never came back out.

One of the children stayed back there with him all the time. They took turns spending the night with him. They put a recliner beside his bed and rested in that.

My knees had started bothering me real bad and I couldn't wait on him like I would have liked to. The girls looked after him and gave him his medicine and all.

Glenn was with him the night he died. It was the middle of the night and I had gone to bed. Glenn said he died easy; said he just quit breathing.

He died July 28, 1993. He was eighty-seven. I was eighty-two.


One day, back before he had got sick, Odell wanted to find his brother George's grave, George was born November 19, 1898 and died May 21, 1945.

So we drove out to Shiloh Methodist Church on Highway 150 where he was buried. We found his grave. It was just a plain grave, nothing there—no flowers, nothing.

Odell said, "I want some flowers on his grave."

I had some artificial ones at home, so we came back home and got them, took them back out there, and set them on the grave. I don't know how long they stayed on there, but the last time I was out there; there wasn't any on it.

I keep flowers on Odell's grave. I make sure to put flowers on his grave that will last. I tie them on so the wind can't blow them off.

He liked his flowers although he wasn't about to work with them or admit that he liked them.


The children didn't want me to be alone, so Macks stayed with me in the daytime and some of the others stayed of a night. I wasn't afraid, but they stayed anyway.

Fay finally offered to stay the night with me all the time. Her husband, Lonnie, had died and she was free. She lived in a trailer next to me and it was getting old.

So, one day I said, "Well why don't you come on down and move in with me."

She thought a little bit and said, "I just might do that."

Within a week she had moved in. It has worked out well.


Saturday night, November 5, of 1994 Glenn called me and told me that they found Macks laying in the yard of his house.

Said, "He didn't make it."

That's the way they give it to me.

Tootsie, Macks' wife, was working that night and wasn't home. Their grandson, Derrick, was living with them, but he was visiting with his mama. When Derrick came home he couldn't find Macks, or anybody. Since it was so late Derrick got worried and called Kay. Kay didn't know anything about where Macks was. She told Derrick to look around again to see if he could find him.

Derrick went looking around and found him outside on the

ground. Phone calls were made to Foster, Glenn and Linda to come. They knew when they saw Macks that he was probably dead. Nurses at the hospital said he never knew what hit him. We still don't know exactly what it was that killed him. Nobody knows.

Macks had been up here at the house that Saturday morning. He had been to an auction sale.

Some said, "He can't be dead; I just saw him at the auction sale."

When Macks died, it was harder than Odell. I knew Macks wasn't well, sometimes when he was working around the house or the yard I could tell something was wrong, but I didn't know he was that sick.


Frances died in 1985. She had been sick for a while with a bleeding ulcer and wouldn't go to the doctor like she ought. One day she passed out at home and they called the ambulance to take her to the hospital. They operated on the ulcer. After the surgery, she got a blood clot on her brain and died. Will died a couple years later. He was living with Linda when he died.

Julie, Lela, Irvin, and Fred died, but I can't remember the years. Cora died a couple years ago. She is the latest one to die. She was still living in Atlanta, Georgia. I didn't get to go to the funeral because of my legs. I've had trouble with my legs for years. I've had one knee operated on.


I still attend Meadowview Reformed Presbyterian Church. Its

beginning attendance of around fifty people has grown to over four hundred.

We've had a lot of pastors come and go, but the one that helped me the most was Rev. Werner Mietling. Rev. Mietling came to Meadowview as our pastor in the early 70's. I was on the pulpit committee. Just before Werner came—while Archie Jones was our pastor—we pulled out of the Southern Presbyterian Church and joined the Reformed Presbyterian Church Evangelical Synod, which later merged with the Presbyterian Church in America.

I can say one thing, I learned more from Werner Mietling than I did from anybody I had ever heard in any church I ever attended. When Werner got here, he got down just like a school, and he taught us from A to Z. He saw we needed it.

He taught the men how to be officers. Then it got so the elders could take over and run things like they ought to. Rev. Mietling left us in the late seventies to fill a position on the denomination's mission board. He was perfect for the job since he and his wife, Jean with their three children Sam, Susan and Margie, had been missionaries themselves in Chile, South America before they came to Meadowview. We all missed them.

# 30

In the mid 90s the state took more of the farm to build a new Highway 52 and Business 85 junction. They built a service road alongside Highway 52 to give access to Business Highway 85, Old Highway 29 South and Old Highway 64 West. Since the service road ran through our property, some of the grandchildren worked and had it named Odell Owen Road.

The new highway came right through the driving range. So Macks moved it north to a piece of land Odell had given him on Odell Owen Road. Macks ran the driving range until he died. His wife, Tootsie, continued to run it for a little while, and then she closed it.

Because of the strong growth in attendance, Meadowview out grew its small sanctuary on Beethoven Avenue. So the church approached Tootsie about the driving range property as a place to build a new sanctuary and she sold it to them. They wanted a little more land than what Tootsie had, so since my land joined hers, I sold them the rest that was needed.

I gave back to God at least half of what I got out of the land, I felt like I ought to, to let him know that I was thankful for it.

The new church was finished in the late 90s.

If any of my life had to be lived over again, I would want it to be the part I lived at Meadowview Presbyterian Church. The ups and downs, the fights we had to keep it together, being friends with all of them. That meant a whole lot.

I turned ninety the year of the new millennium. In my years, I have seen changes my grandparents could never imagine—cars, airplanes, telephones, television, computers, space travel and all the modern conveniences we have that make our lives so much easier. In the last hundred years, I guess there have been more changes in the way we live than any time in history.

By ninety-one I had been in and out of the hospital a few times with a couple spells of heart failure. My sons and daughters are good to look after me. They keep the house up for me and do anything that has to be done. Fay is right here to cook for me and look after me when I need her.

They take me out to eat an all. Nearly every Sunday after church, some of the girls take me out to eat. We like to go to the hospital cafeteria. It's not crowded and the foods good. We see Archie Sink almost every Sunday we go there to eat. He always comes around to speak to us.

We used to go out and eat more often, but I got tired of that. You can't get the same thing out that you can get at home. I don't like things with a lot of salt and most of it has a lot of salt. My blood pressure can't stand that now. Since my last trip to the hospital Fay has been doing most of the cooking. She bought a new frying pan and she enjoys using it.

Now, I fill my days with things I like to do. I like reading mostly. I read my Bible and different books and magazines. I have a new sewing machine. I went in there to use it and couldn't see to thread it, so I've never used it.

When my health gets good again, I'd like to take another trip. I would like to fly out to Washington to see Charlie Warfford. Yes, that's what I'd like to do. That would be nice. Him and his wife always comes by when he's in town visiting relatives. He's been by to see me a couple of times since Odell died. He was here recently, but he didn't get to stay long.


On June 28, 2002 I turned ninety-two; the children gave me a birthday party here at the house. All the children and most all the grandchildren and many of my friends were here—over a hundred people I guess. We had a big cake and they all made over me. It was real nice.

My life is good.

The Lord has been very good to me.

Alma died September 28, 2002, three months to the day after her birthday party. She died at home of heart failure with her daughters gathered by her side. Her death came on Odell's birthday. We all miss her greatly.

Alma Lee Cross Owen